INTRODUCTION

The Beginning of Unruly Figures

When I was in high school, the cool kids didn't like history class. Even when the coolest teacher in our school taught history our junior year, the subject was still only considered tolerable because it meant one hour with the cool teacher who taught it.

I was not a cool kid. I loved history. Even the whitewashed version of history I was taught in Texas public schools was fascinating to me.

When I got to college and started to learn about what really happened, history went from fascinating to all-consuming for me. It manifested in reading memoirs and nonfiction around the clock. I minored in history at Texas A&M, though my major, international politics and diplomacy, was basically a history degree. Later, I went on to get a master's degree in history and literature from Columbia University.

Various advisors and professors actively discouraged me from pursuing a PhD, though, because the future of the history field looked dim. Between the adjunctification of higher education, the dismally low pay, the untenable instability, and the focus on research inaccessible to the larger public, a PhD looked like a good way to see my research languish in pay-walled archives and reach nobody.

I've always felt bad for people who hate history—not because they don't know where they came from, but because they are missing out on an endless amount of dramatic, funny, moving, terrifying stories. The same people that hate history watch *Star Wars* on repeat without realizing that it's just World War II in space. The people who came before us led complicated, strange, funny, beautiful lives, just like we all do. I am always surprised when people can't see that.

I think we're coming around on that. Commercially successful fictionalized accounts of history—like the television show *The Crown*—have helped people see that history is full of strange and fantastic stories. When you look closer, the truth is often even stranger.

I began my *Unruly Figures* podcast to celebrate those strange truths lurking in our shared past. The rebels, rule breakers, and revolutionaries who populate these pages are usually either forgotten or mythologized, sometimes both. But they were real people with doubts and love lives and struggles and successes. They were flawed and funny, beautiful and bewildering. One inspired the Red Cross, the most well-known nongovernmental association on Earth, but he was also terrible with money and bankrupted his entire family—a real ideas guy. Another freed her country from colonial domination, but then tried to install her lover as dictator. A third is remembered as the Magnificent and the Lawgiver, but repeatedly broke protocol for love.

These are the stories in our histories that can't be ignored.

Why These Twenty People?

It might help to think of the twenty people featured in this book as the people whom you would gossip about during lunch. I know, we're not supposed to gossip. It's not nice. But neither were a lot of these people. *Nice* is not going to be the term you use to describe many of the folks here, maybe not any of them.

What they were was determined and daring and dodgy. They were often reckless, sometimes conceited, but invariably they did something that changed their world. They recognized the rules of civility, the boundaries that they were supposed to live within, and simply decided not to.

UNRULY FIGURES

UNRULY FIGURES

Twenty Tales of Rebels, Rule Breakers, and Revolutionaries You've (Probably) Never Heard of

VALORIE CASTELLANOS CLARK

with illustrations by **Sam Kostka**

—•—

PA PRESS

PRINCETON ARCHITECTURAL PRESS · NEW YORK

CONTENTS

*For my dad, who showed me
which rules to break, which to follow,
and how to know the difference.*

I worry about chronicling some of these people who present and represent various ethical questions. Huang Chao is responsible for the deaths of thousands. Suleiman the Magnificent ordered the invasion of other kingdoms and kept enslaved people. Manuela Sáenz unquestioningly supported a dictator. These are all bad things.

It turns out that to be a rebel is not necessarily to be a hero. Our modern love for rugged individualism has cast the two almost as synonyms, but rebellion is rarely clean. The very nature of breaking the rules means that the possibility of pain is on the table. All the people in this book have marks on their record, though some less than others. As a historian, it's my responsibility to make sure that pain is accounted for when I recount their lives. These stories demand honesty, not glossing over for the sake of a more palatable tale.

I chose them because, of all the rebels and revolutionaries who have acted around the world, these are the ones often overlooked. Even those whose names are recognizable—like Jonas Salk—have experienced moments of rebellion that are traditionally left out of their stories. Each historical figure has something to show you about what it means to live life on your own terms, whether you've never heard of them or are surprised to learn something new about an old favorite.

My hope is that encountering their stories will remind you that the people who came before us were much more complicated than we give them credit for. More than that, I hope these twenty people remind you that there are many ways to live life, and that figuring out how to live life on your own terms sometimes looks like coloring way outside the lines. Sometimes, it looks like throwing away the book altogether.

Says Who?

People with motives often trick learners into believing that facts are static. Water is wet, the sky is blue, et cetera. But water can be frozen and made hard; the sky can turn pink and purple at sunset and gray just before sunrise.

Facts can seem obvious, fixed, until they're not. History is just facts that we think are right. We think we know something until a historical journal pops up and proves it wrong, until another lost city is uncovered that reveals another story. It happens more often than you think! The history we have inherited is not nearly as static as we were taught in school.

To wit, you might read a chapter and think, "I don't remember learning that in school!" A couple things could be happening:

1. History taught during K–12 in the United States is often toned down to make events "palatable" for young learners.
2. Archaeologists and historians might have discovered new information since you last took a history class.

I hope you will be open to the way the sands of time shift. This book was diligently researched through archival dives and reliance on experts. Any mistakes within are my own.

Learning and writing about these twenty rebels has been an absolute pleasure. I hope you enjoy reading about them as well.

Kandake Amanirenas

c. 60 BCE – c. 10 BCE

THE ANCIENT KINGDOM of Kush, in modern Sudan, is often overlooked in favor of its more famous neighbor: Egypt. Similarly, Kandake Amanirenas, Queen of the Kingdom of Kush, is often forgotten in favor of another famous queen who tangled with the Romans: Cleopatra. But while Cleopatra married Mark Antony, Amanirenas led an army against Roman invaders, eventually accepting the full surrender of Caesar Augustus.

Kushites resided in a region directly south of Egypt called Nubia. For centuries, the two kingdoms had strong ties. In fact, the Egyptians gave us the name *Kush*; the Greeks referred to the land as *Aethiopia*. The Kushites had a written language, but it has never been fully deciphered and translated. So historians have to rely on outsiders—like the Egyptians, the Greek geographer-historian Strabo of Amasia, and the Roman historian Cassius Dio—to learn what happened in the Kingdom of Kush.

As neighbors, Kush and Egypt were alternately trading partners and military enemies. Like the Egyptians, the Kushites lived along the banks of the Nile, built pyramids for their dead, and worshipped the god Amun and the goddess Isis. The royal families of both kingdoms often intermarried, and around 1500 BCE, Egypt invaded and annexed Kush. When Egypt's New Kingdom disintegrated in 1070 BCE, Kush emerged once again as an independent kingdom. In 773 BCE, the tables turned when Kush conquered Egypt and Kushite kings ruled from Memphis, south of Cairo. Eventually, the Egyptians rose up and pushed the Kushite rulers south again. When Kush itself collapsed in the fourth century CE due to internal strife and external invasion, it was largely forgotten. It wasn't until the early twentieth century, when British archaeologists began uncovering ruins from Kush, that the power and breadth of the kingdom was revealed.

Because of its position between the Mediterranean world and sub-Saharan Africa, Kush was a trading point for luxury goods, especially ivory, gold, and other exotic objects.[1] Gold, which the Egyptians highly prized, was plentiful in Nubian deserts, making the Kingdom of Kush very wealthy.

Amanirenas ruled over this wealthy kingdom as *kandake*, the Kushite word for queen, alongside her husband, Teriteqas, the *qore* or king. We don't know anything about the early years of her life. She was probably born sometime between 60 and 50 BCE, during the Meroitic period of the kingdom, when the royal cemetery was at Meroë. The royal family would have lived in palaces that "looked down on broad avenues lined with statuary while the lower classes lived in mud-brick homes or huts…[but] even the poorest citizen of Meroë was better off than anyone elsewhere."[2] The palace itself would have been impenetrable and the interior decorated in "inconceivable splendour."[3] Amanirenas might have moved about her kingdom "surrounded by chanting priests" and "encased in gold and bright glass jewels…the divine incarnate."[4]

At some point, when is unclear, Teriteqas died. The royal couple had a son, Akinidad, but either he was too young, incapable, or uninterested in ruling, so Amanirenas took on the title *qore* in addition to *kandake*, indicating that she became the active ruler of Kush.[5] The cult of Isis was popular in the region at the time, and Kush had been ruled by women before Amanirenas, so it may have been easy for her to transfer power to herself. A female ruler on her own was still rare in the ancient world, though, so much so that the Greek historian Strabo's account of her depicts her as a "masculine woman."[6] The Greeks tended to look down on female rulers as signs of a degenerate civilization, so his account is accordingly biased against her.

From the capital at Meroë, Amanirenas watched as the Roman armies advanced into Egypt in 30 BCE and defeated Cleopatra. Once Egypt was subdued, Caesar Augustus and his prefect of Egypt, Cornelius Gallus, began to look toward Nubia. Just a year later, Gallus marched south and conquered Philae, an island on the edge of Nubia. The rulers of Kush weren't pleased but held their line, refusing to engage militarily. Gallus began erecting monuments to himself, celebrating his achievements in Latin, Greek, and hiero-glyphic Egyptian. According to historian Cassius Dio, "Gallus set up images of himself practically everywhere in Egypt, but also inscribed upon the pyramids a list of his achievements."[7]

Gallus was eventually removed from his position in Egypt because "he indulged in a great deal of disrespectful gossip about Augustus and was guilty of many reprehensible actions besides."[8] It is possible that some of the "reprehensible actions" Dio mentioned could include provoking the Kingdom of Kush. That might explain why Strabo's account includes the curious line that the Kushites "did not know who Caesar was," despite their grievances against him.[9] Perhaps the war that follows was retaliation for an action Gallus took that has been lost to time.

In 25 BCE, with Prince Akinidad safe in the capital, Kandake Amanirenas herself led a Kushite military expedition of thirty thou-sand men north to Egypt. The Egyptians referred to Kush as the Land of the Bow, and we can assume that many of the soldiers Amanirenas took with her were archers. It was a perfect moment for a preemptive strike: a large portion of the fifteen thousand Roman troops stationed on Egypt's southern border had been pulled away by Aelius Gallus (no relation to Cornelius Gallus) to conquer Arabia.[10]

Amanirenas's men invaded Thebes, "ravaging everything they encountered," and attacked the Roman garrison at Syene.[11] They took Syene, Elephantina, and Philae, where they "enslaved the inhabitants, and threw down the statues of Caesar."[12] As proof of their victory, they removed the head of Caesar Augustus from one of his many statues and carried it back to their capital at Napata along with their captives. A contemporary carving depicts Amanirenas holding two swords and feeding her Roman captors to her pet lion.[13]

However, Augustus's new prefect of Egypt, Gaius Petronius, mustered up a force of ten thousand infantry and gave chase. He reclaimed the cities and sent an army to Napata, crushing the capital and killing hundreds of people. "This place was razed to the ground," according to Dio.[14] Several thousand Kushites were captured and sold into slavery; about a thousand were sent directly to Caesar, probably for sacrifice in the bloody Roman games.[15] The fate of Prince Akinidad is not clear; it's possible he died during the invasion.

Amanirenas and her army were not there in Napata, however; they had already retreated to the city of Pselchis. But what must have been a devastating loss for her did not frighten her into surrender.

What happened next is a matter of historical debate. Some say Petronius pursued Amanirenas to Pselchis; others say he withdrew after crushing Napata, and Amanirenas's army pursued him back into Egypt. Nevertheless, the armies engaged again, each sustaining losses. Some accounts say that Amanirenas rode trained war elephants into subsequent battles. Others say that during these battles Amanirenas was severely injured and lost one of her eyes.

Tracing the exact movements of these battles—which came to be known as the Meroitic-Roman War—is challenging because the records containing the Meroitic perspective haven't been deciphered. There are probably several skirmishes we don't know about and won't until we unlock the Meroitic language. The records we do have are invested in making the Romans look good. Strabo's version of the story is a prime example of this; he frames the outcome of these battles as a Roman victory.

But other Roman records undermine his version. According to Cassius Dio, Petronius couldn't continue fighting "on account of the sand and the heat." The further south the Romans tried to penetrate, the more their supply lines were stretched and the more the heat of the equatorial region made fighting difficult. It's possible that Augustus, fighting several wars at the same time, wasn't willing to send more resources to Petronius to ease this war for him. After a few years of fighting like this, Petronius "compelled" Amanirenas to begin peace negotiations.[16]

Strabo's less biased version of the story suggests that Amanirenas's troops trapped the Roman army in Premnis, a hilltop city that the

**Amanirenas led
an army against Roman
invaders, eventually
accepting the full surrender
of Caesar Augustus.**

Romans had fortified as a military outpost. The Romans' canons could fire "deadly darts over long distances" and made any "assault by Queen Amanirenas nearly impossible."[17]

Yet Petronius was surrounded. He could neither escape nor fight. He was outnumbered and running out of supplies; he had amassed only four hundred men and two years' provisions in Premnis.[18] Again he compelled Amanirenas to begin peace negotiations. In this retelling, the Meroë warriors joke that they can't negotiate because they don't know who Caesar is or where to find him. Petronius gave them escorts to Augustus's palace on the Greek island of Samos so they could meet with Caesar.

Amanirenas didn't go to Samos herself. Instead, she sent envoys with a gift: "a bundle of golden arrows, and, according to legend, this aggressive message: '*The Candace [kandake] sends you these arrows. If you want peace they are a token of her friendship and warmth. If you want war, you are going to need them.*'"[19]

In 20 BCE, Amanirenas's diplomats and Caesar Augustus signed the Treaty of Samos, in which the Romans made two large concessions. The first was that they canceled a tax on Meroë, which had probably been instituted when Gallus conquered Philae.[20] The second redefined borders between Roman-occupied Egypt and Kush.[21] The Romans retreated back nearly to the original Egyptian border and designated a neutral buffer zone where Romans and Kushites could mix peacefully.[22]

While some details of the treaty are unclear, it indicates clearly a victory for the Kingdom of Kush. Nubia had long been a highly contested area because of its natural resources; that Amanirenas retained control over Nubia signals that she was the victor. Even Strabo admits that Amanirenas and her ambassadors "obtained all that they desired" in this treaty.[23] The treaty ushered in a three-hundred-year period of peace.[24] Rome never extended south past Egypt, nor did the Kushites invade Egypt again. Instead, both kingdoms benefited from increased trade.

The Kingdom of Kush had many female monarchs throughout its history. The *Encyclopedia of Black Studies* suggests that *kandake* iconography implies that they were "considered divine rulers, as they are positioned at the same height as and next to the primary deity of Meroë, the lion god Apedemak."[25] Solange Ashby, Egyptologist at UCLA, noted that images of Meroitic queens like Amanirenas show that femininity and military prowess were not considered mutually exclusive for the Kushites. Depictions show *kandakes* who are "really voluptuous" but also clearly "badass warriors, and there's no question about their willingness to engage in violence. We see these powerful women being depicted in aggressive poses."[26]

In 10 BCE, Amanirenas passed away, leaving her kingdom to Amanitare, another ruling *kandake*. This continued a line of several female rulers in Meroë who were not defined by their relationships with men. The kingdom continued for a few centuries, remaining a wealthy and independent nation. It eventually declined due to depletion of natural resources and invasions; by 350 CE, the Kingdom of Kush was over. For centuries thereafter, it was largely forgotten.

In 1910, the bronze head of Caesar was found during excavations in Meroë. It had been buried underneath the steps to the entrance of a temple dedicated to Amanirenas's military victory over Caesar. The temple is decorated with art depicting kneeling enslaved people, including some dressed in Roman military dress, probably referring to Amanirenas's victory. According to David Francis of the British Museum, burying the head "ensured that everyone who entered the building would trample this image of the emperor Augustus beneath their feet, thereby ritually perpetuating the Meroïte victory over the Romans" every time they went to worship.[27] For Kandake Amanirenas, stepping on the entrance stone probably acted as a reminder of her triumph over the man reputed to be the most powerful in the world. Today she retains her legacy as one of the few rulers to successfully resist Roman incursions.

Huang Chao

unknown – July 884

THE EARLY TANG dynasty was a time of the Chinese empire's international power and increased wealth. But the dynasty was inaugurated in bloodshed by Li Shimin, who killed his brothers and nephews to declare a new royal line. This violent origin would come back around to see the downfall of the dynasty. Huang Chao was one of many revolting against ineffective rulers at the end of the Tang era. Huang's rebellion was brutal, long, and unsuccessful, but it contributed to the fall of the Tang.[1] Like many who step outside the lines, Huang did things that today we consider distasteful and downright criminal. But his rebellion weakened a despotic and bloated dynasty, creating the conditions that allowed a later rebel, Zhu Wen, to depose the Tang's final emperor and set in motion the Five Dynasties and Ten Kingdoms periods of Chinese history.

Many consider the Tang dynasty (618–907 CE) China's golden age. The capital city at Chang'an (present-day Xi'an) was the most populous city in the world with close to three million people living in and around the city; those people lived in relative ease. Situated in North China, near a bend in the Yellow River, Chang'an was a perfect outpost for the empire's expansion from the coast inland. The Tang era was a time of huge growth of commercial connections, religious freedom, international relations, and territorial growth; many far-flung states paid tribute to the Tang court. It was also an age of artistic creativity when literature, poetry, painting, and ceramics flourished, leaving future generations with a rosy picture of the Tang as a romantic era of peace and prosperity.

But peace rarely lasts long.

The period of Tang rule in China can be divided into two distinct parts: Before and after the An Lushan Rebellion in 755, which occurred at almost the chronological half-point of the dynasty's existence. The early period of "grandeur and prosperity" lasted 137 years; the years after the rebellion experienced "ruin and disorder, which lingered on for 151 years."[2]

Historian Ray Huang credits the Tang's ongoing rebellions and downfall to the increased indolence of the dynasty's central leadership. An Lushan was a Chinese general of Iranian and Turkish descent who became a warlord during the ineffectual reign of Emperor Xuanzong; in 752 An rose up and declared himself emperor. Even after his rebellion was put down and the Tang government recovered some power, China wasn't the same. Tibetans revolted; peasant rebellions and warlordism erupted throughout the provinces; eunuchs deposed emperors; Buddhist monasteries expanded their wealth and power. Meanwhile, Tang bureaucracy expanded until the dynasty began to collapse under its own weight; money was wasted on "more than 20,000" musicians and performers at the palace in Chang'an alone.[3] Various Tang rulers responded to each issue with a heavy hand of persecution. For example, in 845 Emperor Wuzong destroyed 4,600 Buddhist temples.[4] According to historian Ray Huang,

The tragedy of China was that the unification of an enormous empire was realized before local institutions and technological capacities had an opportunity to develop and mature. The lack of functional capability at the middle echelon deprived the government of an effective grip, for which despotic rulers had to compensate with their personal vigilance.[5]

Inefficient administration and a growing population led to the breakdown of government systems. Economic growth couldn't be monitored, a once-generous government-administered land-allotment practice became infeasible, local rule was consolidated under military figures rather than government administrators, and heavy taxes began to burden the dispossessed working class. On top of the human mistakes, years of flooding and resulting famines along the Yellow River made the population desperate. The closer to Chang'an a Chinese city was, the more oversight the administration was capable of. But in far-flung territories, especially to the north, warlords began to rise.

Eventually, violence spread into central China. One of these rebellious warlords was Wang Xianzhi, who in 874 cultivated an army of disgruntled Chinese citizens and led them against the local military leaders. One of his lieutenants was Huang Chao.

Huang's early life is shrouded in mystery. Early Chinese biographies of him directly contradict one another, so it's hard to know what to believe. The undisputed facts are few, and only one is part of his early life: Huang was born in the province of Shandong. He could have been born around the 840s or maybe early 850s.

It's often suggested that he was well educated and sat for the famous Chinese annual civil service examinations but failed. Failure was common—only around 1 percent of sitters passed the exam—and he could have retaken the exam as many times as he wanted.[6] Instead, he possibly became embittered against the Tang rulers because of his own failure and did not retake the test.

Frustrated, he might have gone into the salt trade. Some accounts say that his family members were wealthy traders and he joined the family business; others say that he began illegally smuggling salt at this point. Salt was a monopoly controlled by the government, and leaders artificially inflated salt prices as a reliable source of revenue for the bloated administration. Inflated salt prices accounted for "more than one half of the state's revenue" by the time Huang was possibly engaging in this illicit trade.[7] Smugglers would undersell the government's prices to farmers, risking the death penalty for their troubles.

This black market would have brought both Huang and Wang Xianzhi into contact with the peasant class. The mutual benefits of their underground business would have forged friendships and the kind of trust that might lead people into open rebellion.

The inspiration for their rebellion is murky. While the Tang government's failures are clear to historians—and were clear to the people living through the time—the moment that convinced Wang and Huang to pick up their weapons is lost to time. Historian Adam Fong suggests the key to the rebellion was bad harvests; the connection between famine and rebellion is well documented.[8] Ray Huang suggests the cause was "the termination of official inefficiency and corruption."[9] It's tempting to cast Huang and Wang as selfless heroes who were defending Chinese peasants against government exploitation—Huang called himself the commander of a "righteous army" whose moral duty it was to "rectify injustice"—but some of their actions make this position hard to defend.[10]

The number of people who joined the rebellion is unclear. Eleventh century estimates claim that 600,000 troops joined the rebellion; but twentieth-century historian Howard S. Levy suggests these numbers cannot be trusted.[11] The figure, he says, probably represents deliberate distortions by the wealthy and landowning classes to incite fear of the masses.[12] However, the fact that 600,000 is an exaggeration is still a signal that the group was probably large—historian Ray Huang suggests it was probably closer to 250,000.[13] Yet other estimates suggest that only 5,000 people had joined.[14] Though the true number is unclear, the rebellion nevertheless gained strength, roiling through the eastern coast of China.

By 878, Huang Chao oversaw his own forces. How this came to be is debated. Many say Wang Xianzhi died and Huang stepped into his role. Others suggest the two split over strategic differences. Nevertheless, in 879 Huang's rebel forces marched south to occupy Guangzhou, an important city center of Sino-Islamic trade.[15] On the way, he converted government troops to his cause, thereby legitimizing his rebellion.

It has been suggested that, at this point, Tang officials and Huang discussed a government position in exchange for peace.[16] Whether the emperor extended this offer to Huang, or whether Huang suggested he might be amenable to dismissing his troops if he were elevated to governor of Guangzhou is unclear. Huang had previously tried to attain a government position; it's possible that he was tempted by this trade. Nevertheless, someone rejected the proposal, and the rebellion continued even in the face of plagues in Guangzhou that killed a large portion of Huang's followers.[17]

Arabic sources suggest that, while in Guangzhou, Huang's followers committed genocide, slaughtering 120,000 immigrants—Muslims, Jews, Christians, and Persians among them.[18] Contemporary Chinese historians don't comment on this massacre, but they do mention that Huang's forces trampled the mulberry groves used to feed silkworms; the silk trade out of Guangzhou took years to recover.[19] It's strange that these historians would prioritize counting dead silkworms over counting dead immigrants, but they wouldn't be the first or last to whitewash their country's history.

From his base in Guangzhou, Huang moved north in 880 and captured Chang'an, forcing the Tang leader, Emperor Xizong, to flee east. Huang declared himself the first emperor of the Qi dynasty and installed some of his most loyal followers in high-ranking posts. Otherwise, he kept the late-Tang's bureaucratic structure largely the same.

In the summer of 881, imperial forces recovered the capital from Huang for a few days. The fighting was intense, with citizens engaging in guerrilla warfare against both sides. When Huang quickly recaptured Chang'an, he put thousands of citizens to death as punishment for welcoming back the imperial troops.[20] Several high-ranking Tang military leaders were caught and put to death in the wake of the fighting.

The defeat weakened Tang forces enough that relative peace reigned for at least several months. During that time, Huang tried to settle into running a country. He installed his wife as empress and tried to become a true emperor.

But Huang's mission began to crumble under the same problems that had plagued Emperor Xizong. Due to widespread food shortages and ongoing Tang military presence, he couldn't import food to the capital city. His tentative relationship with the residents of Chang'an disintegrated, and he may have slaughtered many to force peace. Some historians suggest that residents may have been slaughtered as a food source; author Jonathan Clements notes that "a thousand locals a day were slaughtered" and the resulting meat was "euphemistically described as 'two-legged mutton.'"[21]

Meanwhile, the exiled emperor hired Turkish forces to help him recapture his capital. Led by Shatuo Turk general Li Keyong, who had once been a renegade himself but had recently resubmitted to the Tang, the imperial military moved on Chang'an in the winter of 882. Forces loyal to the emperor within Chang'an helped weaken Huang's mission.

War raged over the capital city for a year, with both sides alternately gaining ground and losing it again. In 883, Huang's forces were pushed from Chang'an for the final time. They retreated east, "but suffered continuous defeat and decimation."[22] Only the death of Huang in July 884 put a stop to the power struggle.

As with every part of Huang's story, his manner of death is heavily debated. A defiant suicide in the face of defeat and a beheading by government officials are the two most listed causes. Some allege that Huang told his nephew,

> I wished to exterminate the disloyal ministers in the nation, and to purify the court. After completing these matters, I did not retire. That was indeed a mistake. If you take my head and offer it to the Son of Heaven, you may attain wealth and eminence.[23]

In this telling, he then tried to commit suicide and was decapitated by his nephew.[24]

Ultimately, Huang Chao's rebellion was unsuccessful in terms of establishing a Qi dynasty with Huang as the first glorious emperor. In his attempt at ruling, thousands of peasants had died and Chang'an was destroyed, proclaimed "a dead loss" and "stripped for parts."[25] Once the greatest city in the world, capital of China for over a thousand years, Chang'an was unceremoniously abandoned. Today Xi'an stands in its place.

The Tang dynasty limped along until 907, when another rebel, Zhu Wen, deposed its last emperor and set in motion the Five Dynasties and Ten Kingdoms period of Chinese history. Zhu Wen's rise would not have been possible without the destabilization and discontent that Huang Chao's rebellion inflamed.

Throughout history, Huang Chao's story has been alternately valorized and demonized by Chinese rulers. President Chiang Kai-shek condemned him as one of the "most notorious brigands in Chinese history."[26] But Mao Zedong praised him as "an early champion of the rights of the masses."[27] The truth, like most historical truths, probably falls somewhere closer to the middle. Seeing a bad situation, Huang Chao did what he could to improve it while simultaneously trying to fulfill his own dreams of power and influence.

al-Sayyida al-Hurra

1485 – unknown

IN THE EARLY sixteenth century, European Christians had an intense force to reckon with: the Barbary corsairs. Corsairs were North African pirates or privateers, depending on your perspective. They were feared in Europe, for they attacked shipping vessels and often raided coastal towns to kidnap and enslave Europeans. Their attacks were part of a much larger fight between western Europe and West Asia that had been raging since the beginning of the Crusades four hundred years before, and Europeans were hardly blameless in the conflict.

Into this mix a new power rose from Morocco: a pirate queen who ruled alone and was intent on revenge against Spain. She was known as al-Sayyida al-Hurra.

Al-Sayyida was born around 1485 in Granada, Andalusia, in modern-day Spain. Her parents were Andalusian nobles Ali ibn Rashid al-Alami and Lalla Zohra Fernandez, who had converted from Christianity to Islam to marry Ali. In 1492, Catholic monarchs Isabella I of Castile and Ferdinand II of Aragon conquered Granada, finishing a centuries-long mission by Europeans to recapture the Iberian Peninsula from the Ottomans. Ferdinand and Isabella began a series of forced conversions of Muslims and Jews, which resulted in many families fleeing across the Mediterranean to North Africa. Among them was al-Sayyida's.

The family settled near a military outpost in the Rif in northwest Morocco. Protected by peaks on all sides, this mountain range was an ideal refuge for people escaping a war. Al-Sayyida's father, who had helped found the fort during the Portuguese incursions into Morocco several years before, became the emir and called the emerging city Chefchauoen.[1] He opened the gates to wave after wave of Andalusians fleeing Spain.

While living in Morocco, the young al-Sayyida received an education "supervised by the best-known scholars in Chefchaouen."[2] Her family lived in relative peace, but she never forgot the fear and violence of being exiled.

In 1510, she married into another great Andalusian family living in exile. Records are vague—the only name given to her husband is al-Mandri, which could indicate a man who was both the founder of nearby Tétouan and her father's friend. This al-Mandri would have been at least thirty years older than her though, and by some accounts he died in 1505.[3] It seems much more likely she married his nephew Mohammad al-Mandri, uniting the families as a major political power in the region.[4]

Al-Sayyida became the co-ruler of Tétouan, a city nestled in the Rif with access to a port on the Mediterranean Sea—one of the only ports, in fact, that hadn't already been destroyed or captured by the Spanish or the Portuguese. Conflicts between Tétouan and Portugal were frequent but often interrupted by negotiations; in managing these conflicts she may have "gained her expertise in the intrigues of politics."[5] She began to rule outright when her husband went to battle against Portugal. This level of trust placed in her by her husband and male relatives was common among the Andalusians and Moroccans.[6]

Together, al-Sayyida and her husband restored Tétouan to glory, building a bustling metropolis full of "mazelike streets to ward off invaders."[7] Today, the city is a UNESCO World Heritage Site.

In 1515 or 1519, al-Sayyida's husband died, and she became the sole ruler of the region. It was then that she gained the title *al-Hurra*, a woman who exercised power.[8] In the few surviving records from the time, al-Sayyida is portrayed as "strong, strong-willed, intelligent, well-educated, daring, and brave."[9] Whether she seized power after her husband's death or whether the transition was planned and peaceful, the residents of Tétouan seemed to accept her happily.

Under her rule, Tétouan's prosperity and power grew, especially after she contacted the famous corsair Khayr al-Dīn, better known in the West as Barbarossa or Redbeard, corsair and admiral of the Turkish fleet under Suleiman the Magnificent.

Stories of the corsairs are full of myth, rumor, and legend. But we know some things for sure—the corsairs were based mainly out of the ports of Algiers, Tunis, and Tripoli. They were also more often privateers than true pirates; that is, these sailors worked with local rulers for legal licenses to pillage other ships in exchange for 10 percent of their profits.[10] Through these arrangements, they could attack any non-Muslim ships, "particularly ships from countries with which the empire was at war."[11] Corsairs had free access to licensing the kingdom's ports in order to sell wares and repair damaged ships, but they could also be called on to fight in naval battles against the Christian empires trying to take over North Africa. It was a steep trade-off for a license. Many corsairs were European-born sailors who had moved to North Africa to acquire a privateering license, a fact left out of most European histories of the corsairs.[12]

Al-Sayyida may have made contact with Barbarossa through his charitable work ferrying Muslim refugees from Spain to North Africa between 1505 and 1510.[13] Whether the two actually met then or whether she simply used this connection for an introduction is unknown, but they became linked in history after 1515. Author Laura Sook Duncombe writes that al-Sayyida "obtained some tips on the business of privateering" from Khayr al-Dīn; Fatima Mernissi refers to them as "allies," which suggests a closer relationship than a single meeting. It's possible al-Sayyida and Khayr al-Dīn agreed to split the Mediterranean in half—he was active in the east, closer to the Ottoman center of power, and she in the west, closer to the Spanish ships she targeted.

The peak of al-Sayyida's privateering career was her raid on Gibraltar in 1540. At that time, Gibraltar was ruled by Charles V, the Holy Roman Emperor and King of Spain. In the eighty years since the Spanish had captured the city, its defenses had been allowed to crumble away. When al-Sayyida's fleet arrived, it found "the entire southern flank of the city unprotected."[14] The corsairs were able to attack easily, and "they took much booty and many prisoners," according to Spanish documents.[15]

Did al-Sayyida start privateering to get revenge on the Spaniards who had unceremoniously forced her from her birthplace? That's the story most people tell. According to Mernissi, "Conducting expeditions against the Spaniards became the obsession" of many brave exiles of Andalusia, and "piracy was the ideal solution."[16] Perhaps al-Sayyida was giving her crew an outlet for their rage.

But it's worth noting that North African kingdoms didn't really have navies at the time, due to Spanish and Portuguese occupation of their ports. So al-Sayyida's decision to assemble a fleet may have resulted from her trying to protect North African coastal cities like Tétouan. Or, she may have simply wanted to enrich Tétouan. All these motivations can be true—revenge, protection, and wealth make a heady combination. Certainly al-Sayyida "ensured that the Spanish knew the Moors of Granada had not forgotten how they had been treated."[17] Regardless of her motivations, she was soon known as "the undisputed leader of the pirates in the western Mediterranean."[18]

Whatever her reasons, al-Sayyida assembled a strong fleet and began privateering. She used the money she made from raiding Spanish vessels to enrich Tétouan. The enslaved Christians the corsairs took were either sold in North Africa or freed and hired into the privateering service.

Some historians suggest that al-Sayyida didn't actually sail, but just commanded privateers while she remained in Tétouan to rule. Regardless, al-Sayyida's fleet was the closest thing Morocco had at the time to a legitimate naval force. Her attacks on the Spanish and the Portuguese, who were in turn attacking North African coastal cities, can then be seen as a legitimate form of war. From that perspective, she was "a defender and revitalizer of her city and avenger of her people."[19]

The Portuguese and the Spanish considered her a legitimate rival for power on the Mediterranean. European authorities dealt directly with al-Sayyida, who was known as "the person who could get a hostage released or negotiate terms for trade."[20] Some European records cast her as "bad-tempered and harsh," but they were written by her enemies; naturally they wouldn't depict her in a kind light.[21]

However, it's through these accounts that we get most of our information about her. For unknown reasons, she is largely erased from the historical records of Tétouan and Chefchaouen. Her story was long ignored by male Muslim scholars, so historians must rely on the Europeans whom she negotiated with for information.[22] (Twentieth-century Muslim scholars were interested in her and began writing extensively about al-Sayyida.)

Portuguese and Spanish documentation refers to her only as *Sayyida al-Hurra*, dropping the *al-* to transform *Sayyida* into a name. But *Sayyida* wasn't her name—it was her title. *Sayyida* is the female form of *Sayyid*, which denotes a Muslim descended from Muhammad through al-Husayn ibn 'Alī, the prophet's younger grandson. Her family line is illustrious, so the title *al-Sayyida* is most probably a reference to her ancestry, though some translate it simply as *Lady*. Meanwhile, *al-Hurra* denotes a Muslim woman wielding sovereign power, a queen, a title that she was the last to ever use. Her given name is lost to time, though some theorize it might have been Aisha or Fatima—both common names among Andalusian Muslims at her time. It's hard to put much stock in the guess—her given name is just as likely to have been Leila or Maryam. She's often called just "The Pirate Queen."

Perhaps, however, this queen would have appreciated her posthumous prestige. After her life's rough start at the hands of the Castilians, rising to Isabella's level as monarch and becoming a threat to her kingdom is an empowering legacy. Isabella I and Ferdinand II died in 1504, before al-Sayyida's rise, but their children might have made the connection. And she wasn't done rising yet.

In 1541, after ruling the western Mediterranean for twenty years, she married the sultan of Morocco, Abu al-Abbas Ahmad ibn Muhammad. The two had met many years before, when al-Sayyida and her first husband were appealing to Sultan Ahmad for funds to rebuild Tétouan.[23] Had he carried a torch for her all that time? Perhaps. By the time they married, he was apparently so in love with her that he was willing to leave Fez and hold their wedding at her home in Tétouan at her request. He is the only sultan in Moroccan history to have married outside of Fez.[24] If not arranged out of love for her, then this unprecedented wedding locale is a clear indication of al-Sayyida's power in the region, which may have been stronger even than the sultan's.[25]

With this marriage, al-Sayyida became queen of an empire. Phillip II of Spain was reportedly very upset by this marriage because it consolidated power and strengthened ties between Fez and the city-states.[26] He even compared it to the marriage of Ferdinand and Isabella.[27] In fact, some historians consider the marriage a political alliance expressly arranged to shore up strength against Spain to the north and the Saadi Sultanate to the south. After all, even after her marriage, al-Sayyida refused to leave Tétouan. She continued ruling her city in her own right, though one imagines she and her husband must have made their long-distance union work somehow.

But then, just as suddenly as she'd risen so high, al-Sayyida fell. On October 22, 1542, she was deposed by Moulay Ahmed al-Hassan al-Mandri, her son-in-law from her first marriage.[28] Members of the al-Mandri family had begun collaborating with the emerging Saadi dynasty south of Morocco as it grew in power.[29] The Portuguese residents of the nearby city Ceuta had weakened Tétouan with a trade embargo, opening an opportunity for al-Mandri.[30]

We can assume she was stripped of her title, her throne, and her fleet. What happened beyond that is one of history's great mysteries. She probably went to Fez to be with her new husband, the sultan. In 1545, he was taken prisoner by the Saadians. If she was still alive, she might have fled to Chefchaouen to take refuge where she grew up. Some say she died there in 1562, but no one knows for sure.

There's some speculation that al-Sayyida al-Hurra served as part of the inspiration for the character Calafia, a fictional queen in Garci Rodríguez de Montalvo's *The Adventures of Esplandián*, published around 1510. Montalvo was a Castilian author who had been a soldier in Granada in 1492, when al-Sayyida's family was forced out. When he wrote *Adventures* years later, he focused on the wars between Christians and Muslims, casting Calafia as a Muslim queen sailing into battle with an army of women. Calafia has the word *caliphate* at its root, a clear reference to Muslim power.

If al-Sayyida was the inspiration for Calafia, it means she lives on in the name *California*. Montalvo's fictional empire and dangerous queen are said to have inspired the state's name, and Calafia has transformed into the spirit of California. In this context, she symbolizes an untamed land before European invasion. Diego Rivera's mural in the old San Francisco Stock Exchange represents Calafia as the spirit of California.[31]

Regardless of her connection to Calafia, al-Sayyida al-Hurra stands out across history as one of the last ruling Muslim queens. She was forgotten for a long time, but hopefully we're just beginning to relearn her story.

Suleiman the Magnificent

November 6, 1494 – September 6, 1566

I N THE LATE fifteenth century and middle sixteenth century, Christian Europe and the Muslim Mediterranean were simultaneously rediscovering old texts and the prophetic wisdom hidden within them. The Muslim world especially waited for what is known in Islam as the Last Days, a time of upheaval and "renovation (*tajdīd*) that would compass religious and political institutions, and establishment by conquest of a universal [Muslim] empire...at the end of history."[1] In Islam, ten is an auspicious number, so when Suleiman I, son of Selīm I, became the tenth Ottoman sultan born in the tenth Islamic era, he was seen as the ruler and conqueror who could fulfill this prophecy. Even in his own time, he was referred to as the Master of the Auspicious Conjunction, and great things were expected from the handsome young ruler.[2]

It may seem strange to put a cosmically ordained ruler in a book about rule breakers. Can one be a rule breaker when one gets to make the rules? Suleiman's honorifics might make his inclusion especially confusing—while he's known as Suleiman the Magnificent in European Christian history, the Ottomans called him Süleyman the Lawgiver. So, what makes him unruly? Well, despite being responsible for the consolidation of laws in the Ottoman Empire, flouted convention at several turns.

He ascended to the throne upon the suspicious death of his father in 1520. Until then, his life had largely followed the conventions of princely boyhood in the early sixteenth century. He studied the Koran, arithmetic, music, and literature. Ottoman princes were traditionally taught a trade, so trained as a goldsmith, where he gained an appreciation for jewels and finery.

Suleiman's father, Selīm, became sultan when Suleiman was seventeen years old. As training to take over the throne, Suleiman was made the governor of Manisa, on the Aegean Sea in present-day Turkey. Though Suleiman was his only living son, Selīm reportedly tried to kill him with a poisoned shirt a few years later. Suleiman's mother,

Hafsa, was suspicious of Selīm and made someone else touch the shirt first—the unfortunate man "collapsed at once."[3]

Patricide, fratricide, and filicide were common practices to consolidate power at this point of Ottoman rule; Selīm had probably killed his own father, Sultan Bayezid II. Bayezid was said to have died of natural causes "helped along…by poison."[4] Did Suleiman, or someone close to him, kill Selīm in turn? The historical record is unclear.

Suleiman was twenty-five years old the day he put on the sword of Osman, the sword of state used in the enthronement ceremony for all the sultans of the Ottoman Empire. He was described by his contemporaries as "tall but thin, with a delicate complexion."[5] In addition to being intelligent and calm, the young sultan was known as "a pious Muslim, but completely unfanatical."[6] He established that his rule would be in direct opposition to his father's "long reign of terror" within the empire.[7] (Selīm is remembered as the Grim, and was known for executing nearly thirty thousand of his own citizens and seven of his own grand viziers.[8] His name was used as a curse for centuries.)

After his enthronement, Suleiman quickly began patronizing the arts and encouraging the rebuilding of Istanbul, leading the Ottoman Empire into a golden age of cultural development. He encouraged religious tolerance across the entire empire, especially for Jews fleeing Christian Europe, rendering Istanbul a haven for Jews escaping religious persecution in Europe. However, Suleiman also began expanding the empire's borders, capturing Belgrade within the first year of his reign.

He brought Ibrahim Pasha—who would be at the center of controversy—with him to Istanbul. Ibrahim was the Greek son of a fisherman who had been kidnapped by pirates during a raid and sold into slavery. Roughly the same age as Suleiman, he was presented as a gift to the prince, and the two became "inseparable; they were like one person."[9] On the rare instances that they were separated, they exchanged frequent letters. When Suleiman became sultan, he made Ibrahim chief of his privy chamber, both giving him great power in the realm and ensuring that the young sultan would be guarded in his sleep by someone he trusted. The appointment also guaranteed Ibrahim "the most intimate access" to Suleiman; it was reported that the two frequently slept in the same bed.[10]

It's a common—and valid—criticism of the historical field that same-sex relationships are often erased by historians, rendered as close friendships. A brief scroll through Reddit's "Sappho and Her Friend" or "Achilles and Patroclus" channels brings up hundreds of examples of this type of queer erasure. Sometimes this is responsible reporting—when being queer was criminalized, evidence of the "crime" was usually erased by the people involved; there may be hints, but we genuinely don't always know if a relationship was romantic or not. But with Suleiman and Ibrahim, we know. Erasure by historians in this case is homophobia.

Though Ibrahim held an honored position in the royal household, he was still an enslaved person. Slavery in the Ottoman Empire was a very different practice from American chattel slavery, but the intimacy between the sultan and his slave still raised eyebrows in court. According to historians André Clot and Matthew Reisz, their relationship "was considered such a scandal that chroniclers kept silent about the relationship which, in their view, tarnished the sultan's glory. Most of the evidence we have comes from foreign visitors."[11] Yet even while Clot and Reisz refer to this scandal and relentlessly refer to Ibrahim as "handsome," they never explicitly link the two romantically, contributing to ongoing erasure.

Historian Marc David Baer does make the link. He notes that "despite being married and residing in his own palace, Ibrahim sometimes spent the night with Suleiman I at Topkapı Palace" and that Suleiman occasionally spent the night at Ibrahim's palace rather than his own.[12] This was far outside convention—the only adult male residents of the palace should have been the sultan and palace pages. Ibrahim also had his own room in the royal harem at the Old Palace, another unprecedented privilege. Suleiman's own brother-in-law,

Ferhad Paşa, called Ibrahim the sultan's "whore," a disrespectful but clear definition of their relationship.[13] Clearly, they "violated the convention that powerful men could desire only beardless youths, not other powerful men," creating controversy within the court.[14]

In 1523, Suleiman promoted Ibrahim to grand vizier and governor-general of southeastern Europe, an unprecedented leap from service to the highest offices in the empire. Suleiman built him a lavish palace near the Hagia Sophia and Topkapı Palace. It was on the grounds of the crumbling Greek hippodrome where preceding rulers had showed off their wealth and power with "lavish public entertainments that went on for days at a time."[15] The palace still stands in modern-day Istanbul.

Despite being lovers, Suleiman and Ibrahim wouldn't have had an exclusive relationship in the modern sense. In *The Age of Beloveds*, scholars Walter Andrews and Mehmet Kalpaklı examine a teasing couplet written by contemporary poet Deli Birader Gazali about Ibrahim's love for another man, Çeşti Bali: "It's not that clear who is ruled and who rules these days / It's a wedding feast, so who is dancing and who plays."[16] The suggestion that the powerful grand vizier was under a page boy's spell was a reference to court worries that Ibrahim had too much influence on Suleiman. Indeed, Suleiman's love for Ibrahim made the grand vizier plenty of enemies.

The most dangerous of these was Hürrem. Like Ibrahim, she too had been born abroad—probably in modern-day Poland—kidnapped by Tartars and sold into slavery. In fact, Ibrahim himself may have bought her to give as a gift to Suleiman.[17] Her name at birth may have been Aleksandra Lisovska, but she was nicknamed Roxolana or Roxelane, which means "the Russian woman," though it's often incorrectly translated as "the redhead."[18] She was educated in Ottoman tradition, converted to Islam, and moved into the harem at the Old Seraglio, a separate building for wives and concubines. There, her "playful temperament" earned her the nickname Hürrem, "the merry woman."[19]

Author Laura Sook Duncombe points out that Western under-
standings of the harem have long been flawed—what Europeans
depicted as a place full of "captive slave girls" kept in a prison "where
men could seek any pleasure" is inaccurate.[20] The imperial harem was
"more akin to a sacred space than a prison"; it housed the sultan's
mother, called the *valide sultan*, as well as all of the sultan's children,
their wet nurses, and domestic servants to the women.[21] The palace
may have been the sultan's home and center of political power, but the
harem was often the heart of the sultan's life.

From this center of power, Hürrem captured Suleiman's attention
and held it. The harem had a hierarchy, and usually, he would have
had to visit the women in a strict order. He already had a presumptive
heir by Mahidevran, who was initially considered his most important concubine. In Ottoman tradition, once a concubine in the harem
bore a male child to a prince or sultan, their sexual relationship had to
end—the rule was "one concubine, one son."[22] The mother became
dedicated to training the son to rule, eventually accompanying him
out of the capital to wherever he would be stationed as a governor, as
Suleiman's mother had accompanied him to Manisa. Hürrem overturned this tradition by marrying Suleiman in 1534.

The wedding of Suleiman and Hürrem was the first wedding of
a sultan in nearly a century. Yet Ottoman chroniclers don't mention
this relationship.[23] To marry her, Suleiman would have had to free her
first, which seems to indicate that she had a large amount of influence
over him; perhaps this was why his chroniclers pretended it didn't happen. Her dual roles of wife and mother would have been confusing for
people—at a time when women's lives were dedicated to serving the
most important men in their lives, Suleiman's courtiers couldn't understand how she could possibly serve both her husband and her son.[24]

It would have been traditional for Hürrem to remain at the royal
harem after their marriage, but she used the opportunity of a fire that
had damaged part of the harem to move into Topkapı Palace with
Suleiman.[25] Once she moved in, she never moved out. This brought

a woman out of the private sphere and into the core of the Ottoman political world, previously the domain of men alone. Hürrem and Suleiman's relationship was key in "moving women closer to the center of power."[26]

Despite her unprecedented power, Hürrem was jealous of Suleiman's intimate relationship with Ibrahim. She worried that he loved Ibrahim more than her. Though foreign ambassadors brought her gifts, though Suleiman stopped visiting other concubines, though she was honored as a wife, Hürrem could not tolerate Ibrahim in her husband's life.

After thirteen years as the grand vizier of the Ottoman Empire, Ibrahim suddenly met a downfall. On March 15, 1536, he was found dead in Topkapı Palace. He had been murdered after enjoying a meal with Suleiman.

The circumstances around Ibrahim's death are unclear. Clot and Reisz note, "Torn clothes and bloodstains on the walls—they were still to be seen there years later—made clear that [Ibrahim] had fought valiantly."[27] Others tell a version where Ibrahim was strangled in his sleep.[28] What prompted his assassination is also unclear—had Hürrem ordered it out of jealousy? Had Ibrahim begun to make political mistakes too great to be ignored by Suleiman? Had he committed treason and plotted with the empire's enemies against Suleiman?[29] If there was a known answer at the time, it wasn't recorded.

The man once called *Makbul*, meaning "the favorite," became *Maktul*, "the assassinated." Once Suleiman's "breath and heart," Ibrahim was buried in an unmarked grave that has been lost to time.[30]

Advisers who had once hated Ibrahim didn't like Hürrem much better. Historians often repeat stories that she "poisoned the sultan's mind" and had too much influence on him for the rest of her life.[31] When he later executed Şehzade Mustafa, his thirty-eight-year-old eldest son by Mahidevran, people were outraged and accused Hürrem of inciting the political intrigue that led to his death. A poet of the imperial harem immortalized Hürrem as "a Russian witch," saying that in executing his son, Suleiman "did the bidding of that spiteful hag."[32] In fact, mistakes Suleiman made during his reign were often blamed on Hürrem by his people, and that abdication of fault is partly why he retains his "glowing reputation" today.[33]

Nevertheless, after Ibrahim's death, Suleiman remained dedicated to Hürrem solely. When she died in 1558, he was "completely bereft."[34] As far as we know, he didn't take another lover for the rest of his life. They are buried near each other in their imperial mosque.

Despite his tumultuous love life and the deaths that surrounded it, Suleiman is considered one of the greatest rulers of the Ottoman Empire. He reformed and streamlined disparate regional laws into the *Kanun-i Osmani*, Ottoman laws that would remain in effect for more than three hundred years. He was an accomplished poet, writing under the sobriquet *Muhibbi* (lover). Much of his poetry survives, and several verses have passed into Turkish proverbs. He sponsored a series of monumental architectural projects within his expanding empire, including restoring the Dome of the Rock in Jerusalem. He died of unknown causes in 1566 while on a military campaign in Hungary.

The man remembered as the Magnificent was almost too good at his job—he ushered in a period of Ottoman prosperity that led later sultans into decadence that arguably caused the slow decline of the empire. Prophecies had declared that his reign would be both awesome and apocalyptic, casting him as messianic in his role. He was said to have been accompanied by angels while on the battlefield, and a veritable army of mystics, astrologers, and prognosticators who could help him understand his destiny were given elevated roles within his court.[35] While prophecies of universal Muslim rule did not come to bear, the discussion of end times maybe happened in a more subtle way—in Suleiman's lifetime, the world changed dramatically. The Renaissance was well underway, and the world that had once seemed so known opened up to dramatic new possibilities of governance, religion, conquest, and more.

Aphra Behn

c. 1640 – April 16, 1689

ANY STUDY OF Aphra Behn is really a study of shifting disguises and political guesswork. What we know of her is uncertain, gleaned from the literature she left us. Fittingly for a woman who was a spy for the British Crown, Behn was secretive, and her reputed garrulity did not extend to anything autobiographical for future generations to rely on.

As Behn's biographer, Janet Todd, pointed out, Behn is something of an enigma for us. She was a rare public female intellectual in her era, a genuinely groundbreaking woman—the first woman to make a living writing in the English language. But she was not a feminist the way we would think of one today. Stories of groundbreaking women often reflect a sense of progressive politics, but Behn was a staunch Royalist and bought into ideas of divine right to rule and the dominance of men. Nor did she care much for enslaved people or the other "rabble" of society.[1]

And yet her work daringly explores the equality of sexual desire; she often asked whether women could be rakes as much as men could. "Sexual politics was certainly her subject, but so was sexy politics and political sex," Todd wrote. Behn was always intrigued by the intersection of the political and the personal and explored that confluence in all of her work.

We think Aphra Behn was born Aphra Johnson between 1637 and 1643; most historians land on 1640. According to Colonel Thomas Colepeper, one of the few people to claim to have known her in childhood, her family name was Johnson, and her mother was Colepeper's wet nurse. The relationship between Aphra and Thomas, called foster-siblings, forged by her mother's care would have been an honored one. It could have also helped Aphra gain status, especially during the interregnum between the fall of Charles I and the restoration of Charles II, when social hierarchies were in flux.

Behn was born in Sturry or Canterbury in Kent, southeastern England. Her father might have been a barber and perhaps a "covert" Royalist. As a barber in Kent, he could have exchanged messages with spies newly arrived from the Continent, possibly preparing his daughter for her own adventures in counterfeiting and secrecy. Her education would have been humanist, but not as thorough as the education of boys. Todd notes that she showed a "surprising grasp" of classical languages, history, philosophy, and comparative religions in her mature writing.

Her espionage education might have begun in 1659 when the death of Oliver Cromwell sent the bumbling Sealed Knot secret society into a flurry of activity on behalf of the Royalist cause. Her foster-brother Colepeper and his half brother Lord Strangford were caught up in covert activities. Behn may have traveled to France to liaise with Lord Strangford more easily than Colepeper, who was being watched, or may have served as a cover for letters exchanged between plotters.

There's no proof as such, but it lines up with a later known assignment: her time as a spy in the Low Countries—Belgium, Luxembourg, and the Netherlands. She was sent there for Charles II in 1666 by Thomas Killigrew, the dramatist heading up the King's Company troupe and secretively working in intelligence for the King. This was during the darkest point of the English war with Holland, so Behn could have landed this precarious role only if she'd been able to prove that she had previous espionage experience.

A version of Behn's life story says that she was one of the children of John Johnson, a gentleman who was appointed lieutenant general of Surinam, a short-lived English colony in what is now Suriname, South America. Johnson died during the transatlantic voyage to his appointment, which meant his widow and his children—Aphra and her brother and sister—were temporarily stranded in South America.

That Behn went to Surinam is not in question; the descriptions of the colony in her most famous novel, *Oroonoko,* are too detailed for her to have gleaned them only by reading other people's reports. How Behn ended up in Surinam is up for debate though. Crucially, there is no record of a Johnson destined for a high office in Surinam, nor any Johnsons among the recorded settlers.

Todd argues that Behn probably went to Surinam as part of a spying mission for King Charles II. She might have been recommended to him by Killigrew. This would explain why, on her return to England, she had an audience with the king to "give him 'An Account of his Affairs there,'" an incredibly unusual outcome for a young woman's family trip to South America.

Regardless of how and why she was there, Behn was profoundly impacted by Surinam. With few friends and more time on her hands than usual, she began writing. Possibly she was already considering plays or translations as sources of income in case she could no longer engage in spy craft due to age, shifting political tides, or notoriety. In Surinam, she probably wrote her play *The Young King*, a tragicomedy of heroic lovers in Arcadian pastoral settings, though the play wasn't staged for at least fifteen years after her return to England.

On her way back to England from Surinam in 1664, Behn met the husband whose name she used for all her writing: a Dutch merchant named Johan Behn. The marriage was not a happy one; Mr. Behn seems to have been bad with money. After a year, either he died or the couple split—Todd points out that it was easy to "lose a spouse" in a time of bad recordkeeping.

Soon after this lost spouse, Killigrew sent Behn to the Netherlands as a spy. Her mission on behalf of the English king was to meet with William Scot, the exiled son of an executed republican who claimed to have information for the Royalists about a Dutch-sponsored uprising in England. She was to assess what information he had and whether it was worth anything. Behn and Scot had had something of a romance during her time in Surinam, which Killigrew knew of and was happy to exploit for the king's gain.

This mission is notable not only because it was exciting but also because it marks Behn's entrance into recorded history. Letters she exchanged with Killigrew and other government agents survive, as do testimonies from other spies she encountered. Now in her mid- to late twenties, Behn is a definitive character, and her story is less speculative.

Though adept at role-playing, she was somewhat naive.... She was also quite talkative and would never be remembered as discreet.

Behn traveled first to Spanish Flanders then on to Antwerp with her brother, a maid, and a Mr. Piers. The last appears to have acted as her cover—she was there to sort out her Dutch husband's financial affairs with Mr. Piers's assistance. She was given a code to memorize for her reports to Killigrew and a promise of a pardon to tempt Scot with.

Behn was ill-equipped for this dangerous mission. Though adept at role-playing, she was somewhat naive. She was a bad judge of character and more easily fooled by false sincerity than someone undertaking a third espionage mission should have been. She was also quite talkative and would never be remembered as discreet.

However, she had many qualities that could have helped her work. She was beautiful and intelligent, described as "tall, well-built, even chubby perhaps, full-breasted, with bright eyes, flowing brown hair, well-shaped mouth, and a small neck." She seems to have made friends easily; she liked a drink, was funny, and was sensual, appreciating beauty in both men and women.

The mission was not successful. Scot was hard to deal with, and Behn didn't have the resources to succeed even if he had been helpful. They both asked for too much from their spymasters and received nearly nothing. It was a plight shared by all Royalist agents taking risks for the Crown. Behn returned to London in May 1667, having had the good fortune of missing the catastrophic Great Fire of London the year before, with little to show from her trip.

Todd, her biographer, suggests that Behn may have made at least one more trip to the Continent in the name of espionage. In the late 1660s, Killigrew became interested in Venice's fight against the Turks. Charles II was interested in helping Venice, but the threat from the Turks was too great to risk doing so openly; spies were needed for negotiations and aid. There are no surviving reports to corroborate that Behn had a mission to Venice, but the nature of spy craft demands secrecy.

Somewhere along the line, Aphra Behn adopted the pseudonym *Astrea* both as a codename for her adventures as a spy and, later, as a pen name. It was taken from the seventeenth-century French pastoral romance *L'Astrée* by Honoré d'Urfé. The immensely long novel centers on a fictionalized pastoral idyll in France during the fifth century, where a young shepherdess and shepherd—Astrée and Celadon—fall in love. Celadon is a perfect lover, but Astrée is "a curious combination of vanity, caprice and virtue; of an imperious, suspicious and jealous nature, she is not at all the ideal creature of older pastorals."[2] It makes sense that Behn would choose such a codename. She would challenge many of the "superficial associations of such a name" throughout her life, and though a lot of her writing relied on pastoral imagery and tropes, she often challenged those as well.[3]

She began writing after her return from the Netherlands. Charles II was always in debt and infamously stingy with payments to his spies, often simply not paying them at all. Behn's stay in Antwerp had left her in immense debt, and she spent time in a London debtor's prison before being released with a patron's help. She had good handwriting, so she began copying for money before looking toward the theater for her next adventure. On September 20, 1670, Behn had her debut: her play, *The Forc'd Marriage*, was staged by the Duke's Company. It was a tragicomedy that ends in two noblemen marrying commoners against their parents' directives, a scandalous concept at the time.

Though *The Forc'd Marriage* was well received, it didn't bring immediate financial success to Behn. However, good reviews encouraged her to continue writing, and over the next nineteen years she explored plays, poetry, short stories, and novels. She became one of the first ever professional writers; authors until this time had been aristocrats, actors, court officials—people with incomes from something else. It was Behn's generation that first saw talents like hers and John Dryden's be rewarded with incomes.

Her writing was usually grounded heavily in Restoration culture. Many of her earliest plays were tragicomedies, as was the popular style. As her playwriting improved with time and practice, she handled her narration with the "knowing and sophisticated tones of a Restoration raconteur, full of cynical asides and wry humor."[4] Behn returned often to the subject of arranged marriage, letting her heroines escape loveless unions in comic but unrealistic ways that allowed everyone happiness; Todd extrapolates that Behn's repeated returns to this well have something to do with her own bad luck in love.

The women in her stories often live in a bleak world, even when they're removed to pastoral idylls. They are forced to manipulate and negotiate through places where men have all the power. Of course, Behn led a similar life working in the theater; calling her a whore would have been only a slightly lower insult than calling her a poetess at the time.[5] It was threatening to men that this female writer was so popular. An essay by Elin Diamond suggests,

> The conflict between (as she puts it) her 'defenceless' woman's body and her 'masculine part' is staged in her insistence, in play after play, on the equation between female body and fetish, fetish and commodity…. Like the actress, the woman dramatist is sexualized, circulated, denied a subject position in a theatre hierarchy.[6]

In fact, Behn's writing was often accused of being bawdy and immoral. She of course defended herself, pointing out in published forewords to her plays that her work was no more sexual than that of her contemporaries like John Wilmot, Earl of Rochester, who was famous for his scandalous affairs and sexual poetry. She knew that it was only because she was female that she was criticized.

Her work explored female sexuality in myriad ways, and in doing so challenged traditional tropes of male/female sexual relationships. Her version of the impotence poem, which was surprisingly common among contemporary male writers, focused on the woman's disappointment over the man's frustration. For a brief period between working as a spy and her fiction bringing in a reliable income, Behn had accepted an income from a male patron; there were sexual strings attached to this money. This time as a "kept" writer meant that Behn knew well the relationship between sex and money. As Professor Paul Salzman points out, her poem "To Lysander" explores "the process which forces women to play out the role of their own femininity as they become objects of exchange in a patriarchal society."[7] Lines like "I hate love-merchants that a trade wou'd drive; /And meanly cunning bargains make" illustrate her cynical perspective of Restoration romance and why her heroines escape these loveless deals; at least in her fiction women could win on occasion.[8]

Even the church was not safe from Behn's thrill of sexuality. According to Todd, within her fiction "church-going is seen not as a chance for piety but as the only sexual resource for a girl in a repressive society." She was so attracted to the ritual, opulence, intrigue, and ecstasy of the Catholic Church that it was never a place of worship for her, but rather one more stage for sex and politics.

On occasion, her female narrators find a solution to the problem between sex and money in love with other women. Her poem "To the Fair Clarinda" suggests that the love of women is a safer bet than that with the popular rakes. Homoeroticism, at least between men, had always been part of pastoral fiction, and Behn had little problem with it. She had "always found androgynous people especially seductive," so it's little surprise that she may have engaged in homosexual affairs herself.

The moody and self-absorbed lawyer John Hoyle is usually considered Behn's "main lover" in her life, but she was also romantically linked with women. A dedication she wrote late in life to Hortense Mancini, Duchess of Mazarine and a mistress of Charles II, is "suffused with greater homoerotic yearning than Behn usually allowed herself"; despite this, the two probably never met. Emily Price, an actress in the Duke's Company, which staged most of Behn's plays, may have been a consummated lover. The relationship wouldn't have troubled the circles in which Behn moved at this point in her life. In fact, the older she got the less sure she felt of the "absolute difference in male and female sexuality." For Behn's pastoral fiction at least, "there was no heterosexuality only sexuality."

Behn relished, more than sex itself though, "the sexual electricity in talk between men and women." Consummation was less interesting to her than foreplay, which she saw as "the writer's business." Yet as she grew older, Behn's love for flirtation risked others seeing her as "ridiculous"; sex and the middle-aged woman did not go together, despite whatever personal sexual awakening she might have been experiencing.

In the 1680s, Behn wrote her most famous novel, *Oroonoko*, which tells the story of the titular young prince of an imagined African nation, Coramantien, and his lover Imoinda. Both lovers are captured and sold into slavery by Europeans but meet again in Surinam. There, Oroonoko inspires enslaved people to revolt and must kill Imoinda, who is a willing victim; he's then executed for her murder. The story was instantly popular in part because of the Behn's vivid descriptions of "the cruel realities of life" in English colonies and the story's depiction of Christian hypocrisy around the slave trade.[9] The English antislavery movement was gaining steam and found her depiction of the enslaved lovers useful to their cause, though Behn hadn't really intended it that way.

Behn's health began declining in the early 1680s. She suffered from aches and pains in her back and limbs, which depressed her. These may have been gout or sciatica, but a formal diagnosis isn't recorded. On April 16, 1689, Behn died. Some theorize she was killed by the "cure" of the illness that plagued her—hefty doses of mercury were in vogue as treatment. She was buried in Westminster Abbey, under her penname, Astrea. On the black marble slab on her grave is inscribed, "Here lies a Proof that Wit can never be / Defence enough against Mortality." She probably wrote this little rhyme herself.

Toussaint L'Ouverture

c. 1743 – April 7, 1803

THE ROILING DESTRUCTION of the French Revolution at the close of the eighteenth century had enormous impacts far beyond France's borders. Strained by their internal upheaval, and later by war with Britain, the French couldn't adequately administer their colonial territories for several years at a time. This inability became an opening for rebellion by enslaved Africans in their colony of Saint-Domingue (modern-day Haiti). When the rebellion erupted, a previously enslaved man named Toussaint L'Ouverture rose to lead it, eventually squaring off with Napoleon I and ensuring the success of the Western Hemisphere's most successful rebellion of enslaved people.

Though remembered historically as the Father of Haiti, his background remains a loose sketch of details. Retracing the history of any enslaved person is particularly difficult, as there are rarely archival records of them and any records that do exist tend to dehumanize them. In L'Ouverture's case, the ongoing lionization and mythologizing of the man means that many gaps in the record have been filled in with speculation and idealized fictions. The frustrating fact is that historians are certain about very little of his life outside of his revolutionary activity. Histories abound with contradictions and projections of each historian's own hopes about the man who rose from enslavement to found a country.

L'Ouverture himself contributed to these mythologizing forces. Throughout his life, he occasionally acted "as his own spin-doctor," ensuring through "carefully orchestrated engagement with the international press" and his own people that he was able to project the version of his life he thought was most important.[1] L'Ouverture was conscious of his own historical importance and probably embellished and edited his story with an eye to his legacy.

We do know that Toussaint L'Ouverture was born enslaved in Saint-Domingue and was given the last name Bréda, from the plantation on which he was born. His father, Hippolyte, had been captured in Benin and endured the horrific Middle Passage across the Atlantic in a slave ship. For a while, it was thought that Hippolyte had been a prince of Benin, the second son of an African chieftain named Gaou Guinou. Today it's largely believed that he was more likely aristocratic but not actually royalty. The creation of this royal genealogical mythology might have been an attempt by someone in the family to "reduce the stigma associated with being captured and trafficked into slavery." Upon arrival at the Bréda plantation, Hippolyte married an enslaved woman, Pauline, and together they had six children. Toussaint was their oldest.

According to legend, L'Ouverture was a sickly child and nicknamed Fatras-Bâton, "little stick." Apparently, he defied all expectations by "subjecting himself from an early age to a physical regime that meant he could swim, jump, and ride horses in a way that surpassed the abilities of his peers." He likely spoke Fon, the language of Benin, with his parents and Haitian Creole to communicate with others in Saint-Domingue. Eventually he learned French as well, though his mastery of the language has been debated. As the language of the ruling class, French would have helped him negotiate his revolutionary adulthood. But historians Charles Forsdick and Christian Høgsbjerg are probably right in assuming that he would have "deployed these languages strategically, according to the interlocutor with whom he was faced."

L'Ouverture was a bright child. His father taught him about medicinal herbs and traditional medicine. But his attainment of formal education is often debated. Many attribute his strategic success later in life to a good early education. In a story that L'Ouverture told as an adult, a white colonist in Saint-Domingue once beat him after catching the boy holding a Catholic prayer book; his crime was apparently reading while Black. (L'Ouverture "kept his blood-soaked vest as a reminder and neither forgot nor forgave." He later killed the man.) Yet L'Ouverture's extant writing is often rendered phonetically, suggesting he either never learned formal spelling or struggled with it. Furthermore, he dictated his memoirs, such as they are, in the last year of his life and they are heavily supplemented by another writer.[2] These examples leave us with conflicting ideas of L'Ouverture's formal education. Biographers seek ways to explain how a boy born into slavery led enslaved people to freedom, and many can't believe he could have done it without formal education.

L'Ouverture's dictated memoir is another challenge to substantiating his biographical details. His life story in his own words is not a memoir in the traditional sense. It was dictated while he was in jail and was intended to be a record of his revolutionary actions for the French authorities. For this reason, it reads somewhat like a confession. It doesn't address much of his life before 1791 because that was outside the scope of the French trial. Yet it is often cited as if it is a traditional memoir. And as I'll show, the way L'Ouverture was treated while in his French jail wasn't conducive to accurate or careful storytelling.

We do know some facts. L'Ouverture spent much of his enslavement working with livestock and horses, picking up key veterinary skills along the way. He may have also acted as a coachman. This would have allowed him to travel unimpeded around the colony and would have exempted him from the extreme physical punishments that enslavers were allowed to inflict. Nevertheless, he lived in an environment of casual violence against Black bodies; life expectancy of enslaved persons on the Bréda plantation was just thirty-seven years.

When he was eighteen, he married an enslaved woman named Cécile. They had a few children together, then the marriage fell apart. L'Ouverture later married a woman named Suzanne; it's unclear if he had been widowed between his marriages or if he found a way to remarry despite Catholic rules against divorce.

According to records, L'Ouverture was a freeman by 1776. How this happened is unknown. It was possible for enslaved people in the French system to buy their freedom, so he may have found a way to save up money to do so.

As a freeman, L'Ouverture became a slaveholder himself. Records show that in 1776 he enslaved a West African man named Jean-Baptiste and owned "a modest plot of land." With a son-in-law, he also bought a coffee estate that had come with thirteen enslaved people. The coffee venture failed, and he emancipated some or all the people he had enslaved before returning to the Bréda plantation. There, he resumed his previous work as a freeman.

In the early 1790s, discontent within Saint-Domingue began to boil over. The white French ruling class was experiencing divisions between the rich and propertied elite and the poor but free whites. Within the colonial elite were further divisions between the bureaucrats who represented direct French power and the rich planters who sought freedom from France so they could trade directly with England and the United States. When the French Revolution began in Paris, tensions exploded in Saint-Domingue as well, starting something that resembled a civil war between the white patriots and the white counterrevolutionary royalists.

Similarly, Saint-Domingue was home to an economically diverse population of twenty-eight thousand free Black people. Some were wealthy planters who themselves enslaved people, but many more were made poor by the economic system put in place by the French planter class. All people of color in Saint-Domingue were politically and legally disadvantaged by the colonial government. A complicated series of fights and tension between these five factions—enslaved people, poor free Black people, wealthy free Black people, poor free white colonists, and wealthy free white colonists—began to take its toll on the island.

In the northern mountain forests of the colony, Vodou priests (often incorrectly spelled Voodoo) preached revolution. Inspired at least in part by their French enslavers' egalitarian ideals, enslaved people agreed to rise up on Wednesday, August 24, 1791, while the ruling Colonial Assembly of Saint-Domingue met at the capital of Cap Français (today's Cap-Haïtien). By striking there and then, the revolutionaries would be able to take out the island's ruling class all at once.

A few nights before the uprising, on August 21, while "a tropical storm raged, with lightning and gusts of wind and heavy showers of

"Burn and annihilate everything, in order that those who come to reduce us to slavery may have before their eyes the image of hell they deserve."

rain," leaders of the revolt met for a ceremony that involved "sucking of the blood of a stuck pig" and making final oaths in preparation for war. This ceremony remains symbolically important in Haiti as the starting point of the revolution.

Reality differed from their plans; instead of rising on August 24 as one force, pockets of rebels began fighting early. Across the agricultur-ally developed north of Saint-Domingue, enslaved people murdered their enslavers and burned the plantations. They adopted the slogan of the American Revolution: liberty or death. Seeing the writing on the wall, colonial leaders at Cap Français mustered a force to fight back, though they found resistance among wealthy colonists who wanted freedom from France and poor colonists who felt little loyalty to the colonial power that oppressed them. Despite French resistance, the rising tide of revolution gained force, and by November 1791 about half the enslaved people in Saint-Domingue had joined the revolt, dividing themselves into three armies akin to European military units.

When L'Ouverture first heard whispers of the planned uprising, he initially laid low. Later, his reluctance to join was used as evidence to support allegations that the insurrection was actually staged by the richest planters to scare the middle-class white colonists into compli-ance and that L'Ouverture was initially on the side of these planters. However, there's no evidence to back this up. The theory smacks of racism—it reduces the Haitian revolution to a Shakespearean farce that removes the agency of enslaved people who wanted their freedom.

It's possible that L'Ouverture, a freeman working as a paid laborer for a white colonist, didn't initially identify with the struggles the enslaved people were facing. Forsdick and Høgsbjerg suggest that he "lacked their boldness at the moment of action and waited to see how things would go." Regardless, L'Ouverture got involved in the revolution once he had secured his family's safety away from the battlefields. He joined the movement in October 1791, after fifteen hundred coffee and sugar plantations had already been destroyed and eighty thousand enslaved people were in open revolt.[3] He assumed a leadership role after an early leader, "Samba" Boukman Dutty, was killed in November 1791.

After initial successes, the insurgency stalled. The leaders, unsure how to proceed, approached French leaders and offered to end the revolt in exchange for amnesty and better working conditions. According to the records of General François Kerverseau, during these negotiations L'Ouverture was publicly relegated to an "obscure post" as secretary but actually "served as a puppet master for the whole plot" from behind the curtain of humble acquiescence to French rule. Only when the insurgents' offer for amnesty was rejected did L'Ouverture finally commit to republicanism and "complete liberty for all." He resigned his secretarial post, took on the title brigadier general, and prepared to resume fighting.

With the transition to outright war, L'Ouverture's approach shifted. He began training followers in guerrilla war tactics and united the island's Black and mixed-race people, whom the white colonists had often been played against one another. Though he was close to fifty years old when the revolt started, he actively took part in the fighting. By the end of the revolution, he had been wounded seventeen times in battle and lost several teeth in a cannonball explosion.[4]

Seeing that France was weakened by the triplicate factors of its own revolution, the war with Britain, and the fight in Saint-Domingue, Britain and Spain stepped into the fight to try to make territorial or monetary gains at France's expenses. Spain sent ten thousand soldiers to support the revolutionaries. The leaders of the insurgency accepted their help, but L'Ouverture never fully trusted either the British or the Spanish—he could see that these two slaveholding nations wanted the island for themselves. L'Ouverture knew that allowing them too much power and influence in the revolution would result in his people being enslaved again.

On June 20, 1793, the French civil commissioners in Saint-Domingue, Léger-Félicité Sonthonax and Étienne Polverel, released a proclamation offering freedom to any Black warrior who would

fight for the French Republic against Spain. The edict had the immediate effect of plunging the various political factions on the island
into chaos—in the next three days, nearly ten thousand people were
killed in a struggle over the Cap Français port, all except the revolutionaries ostensibly fighting for the French Republic. When the
fighting ended and the revolutionaries controlled Cap Français, two
things had become clear: the new French government couldn't defeat
the Haitian Revolution, and victory for the revolutionaries might be
achieved through allying with the French instead of fighting them.

The new perspective was borne of the clear fact that the insurgents
were winning. Two years into the fighting, they held major ports and a
lot of territory while white colonists were fleeing to the United States.
The revolutionaries saw this as an opportunity to come to an agreement with France rather than risk that their wartime alliance with
Spain would transition into Spanish control of the island—neither the
French colonists nor Black revolutionaries wanted Spain to take over
Saint-Domingue. However, L'Ouverture was suspicious—the French
had been hypocritically trumpeting liberty and equality since 1789 but
had sent thousands of troops to defend slavery in Saint-Domingue
since then. He couldn't see a reason for that to change and insisted in
a letter to his fellow Black republicans that they were better off with
the Spanish, a partnership that held for another year.

On August 25, 1793, Toussaint Bréda threw off the name given to
him by his enslaver and publicly became Toussaint L'Ouverture. His
new name, which means "the opening," was a symbolic nod to the
possibilities he foresaw in the aftermath of the revolution. Forsdick
and Høgsbjerg note that "L'Ouverture" might have also been a politically expedient reference to the Vodou chant, "Papa Legba, ouvri
barriè pour moins." Aligning himself with the Vodou spiritual intermediary Papa Legba would have helped keep people united behind
L'Ouverture's mission.

The landscape of the fighting changed dramatically in 1794,
when France ended slavery in all its territories. Despite his earlier

misgivings, L'Ouverture knew then that the future of his people was safer under French influence than under Spain or England, as both still allowed slavery in their territories and showed no intention of ending it. So, he turned his back on Spain and allied with the French to successfully push the encroaching Spanish and English forces out of Saint-Domingue.

The dramatic military successes that followed made L'Ouverture widely renowned. Respected by freed Blacks and white European colonists alike, he was made first the Lieutenant Governor and then the Governor General in 1796. Saint-Domingue was still a French colony, but slavery was abolished, dramatically improving the lives of the formerly enslaved people who lived there. L'Ouverture was heralded as a hero, and great things were expected from him.

However, his illustrious reputation quickly began to erode. Early into his rule, he used military discipline to force former slaves to work, though they remained legally free and could share in profits of the plantation where they worked.[5] He also preached reconciliation between formerly enslaved people and their former enslavers; some historians claim this eased racial tensions and others claim it was his undoing. It's a move that easily lends itself to being interpreted through one's personal politics.

After British forces were finally fully pushed out of Saint-Domingue in 1799, L'Ouverture maintained a good relationship with the British despite having fought against them. The French still held the island as its territory, so L'Ouverture "continued to dangle the prospect of British influence in Saint-Domingue as a check against French complacency."[6] In 1798 he negotiated for better trade terms with the British, behind the backs of the French; in 1799 he did the same with the Americans. The two relationships helped the nascent economy of Saint-Domingue recover from the decimating French plantation system and the agricultural damage of the revolution.

In 1801, L'Ouverture sent his forces to attack the eastern portion of Saint-Domingue (modern-day Dominican Republic), which comprised two-thirds of the island and was under Spanish control. Once he ran out the Spaniards, he freed enslaved people and declared himself in charge of the entire island. He dictated a "new abolitionist constitution for Saint-Domingue, asserting that 'here, all men are born, live, and die free and French.'"[7] The new constitution made him Governor-General for life with absolute power, though he claimed he was still a loyal disciple of Napoleon I, who had taken power in France in 1799.

Feeling threatened by this unsanctioned seizure, Napoleon sent twenty thousand men to overthrow L'Ouverture in January 1802; he then reinstated slavery in all French colonies. L'Ouverture instructed General Jean-Jacques Dessalines to "burn and annihilate everything, in order that those who come to reduce us to slavery may have before their eyes the image of hell they deserve."[8] But the French came with more forces than he expected, and by May 1802, L'Ouverture agreed to lay down his arms.

The next month, French General Jean-Baptiste Brunet invited L'Ouverture to a parley under false pretenses. He was arrested and sent to Fort-de-Joux in the French Jura Mountains, where he was jailed without charge or trial. Reportedly, Napoleon's wife Joséphine had counseled him against this move, insisting that it would result in France losing Saint-Domingue forever. "What complaints could you have against this leader of the Blacks?…He has always maintained a correspondence with you; he has done even more, he has given you, in some sense, his children for hostages," she reportedly insisted.[9] (By *hostages*, she meant that L'Ouverture had sent his sons to be educated in Paris in 1796.)

The records of L'Ouverture's imprisonment are a testament to what little respect the French had for him and how severely they were willing to torture him. He was denied his military and political status and forced to live as any other convict. The guards denied him adequate clothing to deal with the freezing winter weather, and though he was clearly ill they denied him medical care. His guard Commander

Baille wrote, "The composition of negroes being nothing at all resembling that of Europeans, I am ill-inclined to provide him with a doctor or a surgeon, which would be useless in his case."[10] Instead, the guards deliberately interrupted his sleep several times a night, denying him any chance at healing. General Ménard, his guard after Baille, proudly wrote that L'Ouverture was becoming "disturbed" as a result; he died three days later, on April 7, 1803.[11] An autopsy attributed his death to stroke and pneumonia and noted that his lungs were filled with blood.

When boarding the ship to his death, L'Ouverture is said to have warned his captors, "In overthrowing me, you have done no more than cut down the trunk of the tree of liberty in Saint-Domingue, it will spring back from the roots, for they are numerous and deep."[12] He didn't live to see the island become truly free. Instead, his deputy Jean-Jacques Dessalines defeated Napoleon and declared full independence from France on January 1, 1804. He renamed the island *Haiti*, a linguistic nod to the Indigenous Taino population who had lived on the island before Spanish contact. Today Haiti remains the only country established by a revolt of enslaved people.

Raḥmah ibn Jābir al-Jalāhimah

c. 1760 – 1826

THOUGH THE GOLDEN Age of Piracy looms large in European and American storytelling, it lasted only from about the 1650s to the 1730s and was restricted to the Caribbean, the West African coast, and the Indian Ocean. But in the 1700s, piracy was rising in another part of the world: the Persian Gulf. A relatively narrow inlet of water, the Persian Gulf is enclosed today by the United Arab Emirates, Qatar, Bahrain, Saudi Arabia, Kuwait, Iraq, and Iran. But in the late 1700s, various powers—including Raḥmah ibn Jābir al-Jalāhimah, a ruler of Qatar—were vying for domination of the area.

Raḥmah ibn Jābir al-Jalāhimah (hereafter, Raḥmah) was born in Grane (today, Kuwait City) around 1760. He was of the Jalāhimah family, one of the Arab clans who made up the Banū 'Utūb federation, which had wrested control of Kuwait from the Banū Khalid Emirate (and later wrested Bahrain from the Persian Empire). Much of Raḥmah's early life is unknown, though he may have participated in these ongoing territorial fights for dominance in and around the Arabian Peninsula.

Raḥmah's father, Jābir ibn Adhbi, became the sheikh (leader of his clan) in the late 1760s. His eldest son, possibly named Abdullah, would have inherited the position from him. Raḥmah, needing an occupation of his own, may have begun earning a living as a horse dealer, breeding and selling famed Arabian horses to wealthy buyers around the Arabian Peninsula as well as to European traders. First imported into Europe about fifty years earlier, Arabian horses had already become prized and were being used to establish the Thoroughbred breed.[1] Through this work, Raḥmah saved up money to buy his first ship and ten enslaved people to help him sail it.

In the late 1770s or early 1780s, the Jalāhimah and Khalīfah clans that had once lived peacefully alongside each other began fighting. Together, the clans had established a free-trade port at Al-Zubārah, in modern Qatar, in the late 1760s. But the Khalīfah clan had refused to fairly share economic gains with their partners, forcing the Jalāhimah to move north to Al Ruwais, also in modern Qatar. Although both cities had ports and Al Ruwais was positioned further into the Persian Gulf, Al-Zubārah had the benefit of reputation. Even after Al Ruwais had been built up, traders sailed past it to trade at Al-Zubārah. Raḥmah, who would have been in his late teens or twenties at the time of the split, seems to have never forgotten the financial loss his clan suffered.

Despite this difficult shared past, the Jalāhimah and the Khalīfah clans banded together to drive out the Persian Empire from the island of Bahrain, located west of Al-Zubārah and Al Ruwais. Without a personal account from Raḥmah, it's difficult to know exactly how he felt about this temporary alliance, but his later actions make it clear that their momentary partnership didn't mean he'd forgiven the Khalīfah for pushing his clan out of Al-Zubārah. The Khalīfah then annexed Bahrain, once again cutting Jalāhimah out of the rewards, which must have enraged Raḥmah. Had the Khalīfah made promises to the Jalāhimah that they reneged on? How did Raḥmah view his father's part as sheikh in these broken promises? That remains undocumented, but it's not hard to guess.

Soon after this second betrayal, Raḥmah and his brother struggled with one another for leadership of the Jalāhimah clan. Raḥmah won and became the sheikh. Some sources say that from then on, the clan used piracy as a means of subsistence living. Women, children, and elderly men probably remained in Al Ruwais while younger able-bodied men took to sailing. However, with the Khalīfah gone and no other dominant power in Qatar, Raḥmah could expand his family's power over the peninsula for a period. He became known as the ruler of Qatar.

We know that Raḥmah established a presence at Khor Hassan, meaning "beautiful inlet." (Today it's called Al Khuwair.) Two curling, offshore coral reefs offshore created a sheltered bay around the city, offering Raḥmah protection from his enemies and a good look-out toward Bahrain.[2] Located between Al-Zubārah and Al Ruwais, Khor Hassan became his base of operations against the Khalīfah. The

Khalīfah had made Bahrain the center of their prosperous pearl trade, bringing them riches and inviting yet more trade to the area. Raḥmah "awaited an opportunity to destroy them."[3] Sometime around this period, he acquired a 300-ton vessel and 350 men to work it. Probably these men were not enslaved but members of the Jalāhimah clan and other volunteer sailors eager for the wealth that Raḥmah promised.

Raḥmah began attacking merchant vessels sailing the Persian Gulf, earning a reputation as "a daring freebooter, without fear or mercy." He preyed on the ships sailing from Persia and Kuwait, as well as the Khalīfah ships leaving Bahrain. During these early exploits, he lost one eye in the fighting and became the earliest documented pirate to wear an eye patch. He avoided conflict, however, with British ships and the Wahhābī, a reform sect of Islam that had attracted a lot of pirates due to its founder's mandate to bring in converts by "fire and sword" and to "plunder and destroy" anyone who disavowed them. According to British author Charles Belgrave, Raḥmah called the British "his friends," though it seems more likely that Raḥmah just didn't want to invite British aggression to Qatar.

When he wasn't pillaging ships, Raḥmah acted almost as a lobbyist. He traveled to various powers along the gulf, trying to persuade them to attack the Khalīfah family in Bahrain. He was always quick to join the Khalīfah's enemies, supporting any invader, meaning that his group of allies was in constant flux.

In 1799, the sultan of Muscat, modern-day Oman, seized Bahraini ships in his port, claiming that they hadn't paid a tax. Perhaps encouraged by both Raḥmah and the Persians, the sultan declared war on Bahrain. Too weak for a fight, the Khalīfah clan temporarily retreated. Battle over the island raged until 1802, when the Khalīfah sought help from the Wahhābī from the mainland, forcing the sultan to back off. However, after driving out the Muscat forces to ostensibly help the Khalīfah, the Wahhābī stayed in Bahrain. In the background, Raḥmah used the pretext of these battles to attack more ships, increasing his wealth and power in the area.

In 1809, Rahmah relocated his base of operations to Al-Dammām, in Saudi Arabia west of Bahrain, after establishing a beneficial partnership with the mainland Saudis. It's possible he sought an alliance with them for a balance of power against the Wahhābī, who had taken over Bahrain. He built a large fort in Al-Dammām, where he and several hundred families lived. He did not yet abandon his base at Khor Hassan in Qatar, though he eventually would. Today ruins of his presence at Khor Hassan can still be seen. Most of the buildings are crumbling, but one octagonal tower, probably used as a lookout, still stands.

In 1810, the Khalīfah clan went on the offensive against Rahmah. Free of the Wahhābī presence and financially backed by the sultan of Muscat after a series of deals, the clan was stronger than before. On a dark night, the Khalīfah found Rahmah's ships at anchor and pulled alongside them in the darkness. According to Belgrave, Rahmah wanted to flee to avoid a conflict but was manipulated into fighting by Ibrahim Faisan, a Wahhābī military leader who had abandoned his people and joined Rahmah's crew of thousands. Against his better judgment, Rahmah stayed to fight.

He led his best ship, *Al Manowar* (a name clearly influenced by interaction with the British), against the enemy fleet. A Khalīfah ship, commanded by the son of the sheikh of Bahrain, pulled alongside Rahmah, and the two leaders engaged in hand-to-hand combat until the young Bahraini was killed and the two ships caught fire and sank. Rahmah's right arm was badly injured in the fighting and never fully recovered. Though both sides suffered losses, this battle is generally seen as a loss for Rahmah. He retreated to Al-Dammām to recover.

The next few years of his life are blank. In 1816, however, Rahmah returns to the historical record when the sultan of Muscat tried to invade Bahrain again. Still not over his grudge against Bahrain's ruling clan, the Khalīfah, Rahmah offered to help with the invasion. But at that moment, the Saudis were at war with the sultan of Muscat. They saw Rahmah's offer to help him as a betrayal and destroyed his fort at Al-Dammām. The sultan's invasion failed, and Rahmah's fleet began temporarily splitting its time between Muscat and Bandar-e Būshehr, on the eastern coast of the Persian Gulf.

There, Rahmah met James Silk Buckingham, who in 1829 immortalized Rahmah in his memoir *Travels in Assyria, Media, and Persia*. Buckingham described Rahmah as "the terror of the Gulf…the most successful and the most generally tolerated pirate, perhaps, that ever infested any sea."[4] He counted Rahmah's followers as around two thousand and claimed that most were enslaved Africans, which is unlikely. He described Rahmah as someone who "affects great simplicity of dress, manners, and living…whenever he goes out, he is not to be distinguished by a stranger from the crowd of his attendants."[5]

If it's true that Rahmah didn't try to distinguish himself from his crew, there are two possible explanations. The first is that he used the disguise as protection against enemies who would have assassinated him. The second is that equality of dress indicated that the captain and crew were equals among themselves, which was the pattern of piracy in the Caribbean.

In November 1819, Rahmah met British Admiral Francis Erskine Loch, who wrote about the encounter in his diary. Loch's description of Rahmah betrays the man's age and how the years of hard fighting had worn him down. He's remembered as

> about five foot seven, nearly sixty years of age, stooping considerably, with a quick waddling gait…wearing a large, black goat's hair cloak, the hood similar to that of the Capuchins, drawn close round his head. Thus his small, but sharp-featured face peered from under the bonnet-shaped hood, giving him the appearance of some hellish old sorceress, rather than the man whose name was enough to create alarm wherever he carried his feuds.

Loch wrote that Rahmah always carried two pistols with him and had developed a habit of playing with them any time he was seated, "cocking them, and half-cocking them, making it not comfortable to be near him, lest the trigger should slip from his fingers." No doubt this was a habit developed to intimidate others.

Loch notes that Raḥmah had an elder son, Bishr, who traveled with him, "a lad of about twenty years of age, of middling stature, rather good looking." Bishr inherited his father's talent on the water and hatred of the Khalīfah. Raḥmah probably intended to leave his fleet to Bishr when he retired, a future that was possible but distasteful to Raḥmah.

In 1819, Raḥmah aided the British forces in their Persian Gulf campaign. Their primary target was the Qasimi clan of Ras al-Khaimah (in present-day United Arab Emirates). Like the Jalāhimah, the Qasimi were piratical and considered the dominant force in the area by some. Raḥmah's exploits are sometimes confused with the Qasimi piracy. He may have allied with them at times out of convenience, but he belonged to a different clan, hence his willingness to aid the British against them.

In 1820, the British and many of the powers along the Persian Gulf signed the General Treaty of Peace. It was intended to end piracy to encourage trade, but no one told Raḥmah about it until after it was signed. He ignored this treaty and continued to wage his wars against the Khalīfah. In 1821, he captured seven Bahraini vessels and killed at least twenty of their men. In 1823, the Khalifahs and Raḥmah made peace, but it lasted only for about two years.

Somehow, Raḥmah found his way into good relations with the Saudis again. He resettled Al-Dammām and built a castle on top of its destroyed fortress. The castle was large, with several towers both round and rectangular. Today, it has completely disappeared, but its ruins were still visible in the 1970s.[6] Raḥmah's followers later expanded beyond Al-Dammām to Katif, modern-day Tārūt Island.

In 1826, Raḥmah sailed for the final time. Sheikh Abdullah ibn Ahmed of the Khalīfah clan was sailing near Saudi Arabia when he heard that Raḥmah was nearby, aboard his ship *Al-Ghatroushah*. The sheikh attacked, focusing several of his ships on Raḥmah, reportedly even crashing his ship into *Al-Ghatroushah* to prevent

From this perspective,
European ships attacking
local powers were just
as engaged in piracy as the
people they accused.

Rahmah from escaping. His ship was boarded, and the two crews fought desperately until "blood ran down the decks and stained the sea around the two ships."

It became clear that Rahmah's men were losing. Desperate and cornered, he blew up his own ship rather than be captured by the leader of his lifelong enemy. Hugging his eight-year-old son, Rahmah lit a keg of gunpowder. With a "vivid flash" and "roar as of thunder," the two ships exploded. Once the smoke cleared, nothing was left of Rahmah or the sheikh.

Much of our English-language information about Rahmah bin Jābir al-Jalāhimah comes from nineteenth-century British colonial sources who had vested interests in presenting him badly. So, when James Silk Buckingham describes him as "dirty," "ferocious and ugly," "brutal," and "savage," we should take this account with a handful of salt. (Buckingham also claims that Rahmah had use of an arm with no bones in it, which is physically impossible, so his account undermines itself.)

Buckingham was writing for a nationalistic British audience who wanted to believe that they were well within their rights to take over Arabia and the rest of Asia. As the British lost colonial holdings elsewhere and battled Napoleon I close to home, it became increasingly important to present enemies of their shipping interests as inferior to themselves. It allowed them to treat outsiders with impunity and take what they wanted instead of negotiating as equals.

Sulṭān ibn Muhammad al-Qāsimī argues in his book *The Myth of Arab Piracy in the Gulf* that many of the documented allegations of piracy were exaggerated to serve British colonial interests. As we saw with the story of al-Sayyida al-Hurra (page 28), "pirate" is a label often applied by enemies; from another point of view Rahmah's actions can be seen as naval warfare between known regional powers and against an encroaching invader. From this perspective, European ships attacking local powers were just as engaged in piracy as the people they accused.

Today, Rahmah ibn Jābir al-Jalāhimah is remembered throughout the Persian Gulf as a folk hero. His exploits are celebrated, and his violent reputation is tempered by rumors that he might have been a poet. When Charles Belgrave lived in Bahrain from the 1920s to the 1950s, serving the Khalīfah family who still rules the country today, he wrote *The Pirate Coast* as an account of the histories there. In it, he noted that Rahmah is remembered fondly "in the markets and coffee shops of the coastal towns" where "old men still tell stories" about him.

Manuela Sáenz

December 27, 1797 – November 23, 1856

MANUELA SÁENZ, BORN in Ecuador in 1797, is remembered as a revolutionary hero in Latin America. She was a friend and lover of Simón Bolívar, the Venezuelan-born political and military leader, and often referred to as the *Libertadora* to Bolívar's *Libertador*. She's widely remembered by people in South America, but many historical accounts, when they include her at all, either reduce Sáenz to a beautiful mistress or downplay her role in the independence of Latin America to a pivotal moment when she saved Bolívar's life. Her story, worthy of a feature film, has become a legend in service to political narratives about South America's march toward freedom at the expense of her personhood. In truth, she was both the love of Bolívar's life and a wily political animal who worked hard for her political goals.

In the late eighteenth and early nineteenth centuries, European Enlightenment ideals traveled across the Atlantic to Central and South America, inspiring new political ideas. Today we call this time Latin America's Age of Revolution. Born in December 1797, Manuela Sáenz was alive at the perfect time to bear witness and participate in this. Her birth was considered illegitimate in an interesting legal way. In Quito, Ecuador, where she was born, her parents recorded her as a foundling child, or *hija exposita*.[1] It means "child of unknown parents," though both her parents were known. It was a designation specially designed to protect the reputations of upper-class people giving birth out of wedlock. That both her parents were considered social elites helped to mitigate the stigma that would have come with being labeled an illegitimate child.

We don't know much about her childhood. Her mother, Joaquina Aizpuru, was part of the wealthy Aizpuru Creole family living in the most prestigious part of Quito. (Creole is used here for someone with mixed Black and European ancestry.) That Joaquina got pregnant through an affair with a married man would have been very embarrassing for the family. Thirty-year-old unwed Joaquina did what social norms dictated she do: she gave birth in secret and handed the baby over to the local La Concepción Convent. Manuela probably never saw her mother again.

Manuela's father, Simón Sáenz de Vergara y Yedra, did have a presence in her life. He was willing to provide for her and even formally acknowledge her, which is how she gained her last name. Though raised by the nuns at La Concepción, she was integrated into her father's family, which gave her the right to be treated as a respectable woman who was to be addressed with the honorific Doña, meaning "madam" or "lady."

When she was nineteen years old, her father arranged a marriage for her. At this time, marriage wasn't thought of as a source of emotional well-being so much as an expedient way to ensure a family's interests. So Simón married Manuela to his wealthy business associate James Thorne, who was much older than her and "one of a small number of British entrepreneurs and fortune seekers who had begun trickling into the Spanish colonies at the end of the Napoleonic Wars."

With this marriage, Manuela Sáenz moved to Lima and became the mistress of Thorne's household, which included command over enslaved people and servants as well as access to fine luxuries. Though the marriage was arranged, Thorne deeply loved her, and we see some of that in the couple's surviving correspondence. In letters he sent her while he was away on a business trip, he called her the "most beloved wife of my heart" and insisted that "a prison, in your company, would be better than a palace."

As an adult, Sáenz was reputedly beautiful but stood out more for her free-spiritedness, generosity, and compassion. She was impulsive and loved a joke. Once, when horseback riding with friends, she appeared disguised as a man in an officer's uniform and fake mustache. She led her friends on a merry chase before revealing her identity.

Over time, she became Thorne's confidant and business collaborator, helping him by conducting business on his behalf. Certain legal and financial transactions—the buying, selling, and freeing of people, for example—usually could be performed only by men, but while

Thorne was away Sáenz emancipated the young daughter of one of their slaves (but not the mother).

Sáenz's life in Lima was surprisingly free, considering the time. Women were allowed to move around the city unchaperoned and could mingle freely with anyone of any class. Women in Lima wore a unique outfit that enabled this freedom and mobility: the *saya y manto*. The *saya* was a long, snug skirt, usually pleated and hemmed to show off the feet and ankles. The *manto* was "a thick veil fastened to the back of the waist; from there it was brought over the shoulders and head and drawn over the face so closely that all that was left uncovered was a small triangular space sufficient for one eye to peep through."[2] The outfit had Moorish origins and probably came to South America with the Spaniards, but it was not popular outside of Lima.[3]

The *saya y manto* was originally designed to serve men's interests: hiding daughters and wives from others' eyes.[4] But women claimed it for themselves and used it to get around the city in disguise. The anonymity it gave them facilitated transgression against the limits that the Catholic Church and the Spanish-controlled government imposed on them. Both agencies tried to ban the *saya y manto* for precisely this reason, but its effective disguise was its safeguard—it was difficult to ticket a woman they couldn't identify, and it was improper to ask a woman to remove it for identification. Even though Sáenz likely had not seen this garment before moving to Lima, she adapted to it, exploiting its obvious advantages.

In the early nineteenth century, Spain was losing its grip on its South American colonies, and anti-Spanish sentiment in Peru was growing steadily. By 1810, "increasingly bitter wars" were erupting between patriots and loyalists. Women at all strata of society played key roles in these battles. Urban upper-class women like Sáenz nurtured the patriot cause by hosting gatherings for discussion of anti-Spanish criticism, giving financial and material support to insurgent armies, and serving as spies, couriers, nurses, and arms smugglers.

Sáenz initially supported José de San Martín, who had won Argentina's freedom and then crossed the Andes Mountains to work against the Spanish in Peru. She recruited men for San Martín and collected donations of clothing to resupply the patriot army.

In April 1822, Sáenz returned to Quito, which would change her life irrevocably: the famous Simón Bolívar was due to arrive there around the same time. Bolívar had already earned the title of the Liberator for his role in Venezuela's revolution. But he was also a conqueror: in the power vacuum that came after the fall of Spanish power, Bolívar had created a Colombian republic that would come to control the combined territories of modern-day Venezuela, Colombia, Ecuador, and Panama. In the same breath that he'd helped drive the Spanish from Quito, he annexed Quito into Gran Colombia.

Bolívar arrived in Quito as its ruler on June 16, 1822. Residents turned out in droves to welcome the Liberator and decorated their homes in red, blue, and gold to symbolize their annexation into Gran Colombia. That night, at a private ball in his honor, Sáenz and Bolívar met and began a romantic relationship. She was twenty-four and he was thirty-nine.

They fell deeply in love. He had had fleeting romantic relationships prior to this meeting but had always prioritized his larger political goals. According to biographer Pamela S. Murray, "He rarely lingered in cities and, when not absorbed in a military operation, was almost always in a hurry to get back to his troops." With Sáenz, things shifted—instead of leaving her behind, he began to bring her with him on his travels. As the years of battle weighed on him, she became one of the few people who could lift him out of his darker moods. Years into their affair, in response to someone's criticism of her impulsivity, Bolívar called her a "dear madwoman."

Thorne learned about the affair and begged her to end it for years, first out of heartbreak and then out of concern for their reputations. She was frank with him, saying that she loved Bolívar and could not be convinced to abandon him. The couple never saw each other again.

By December 1823, Sáenz had become Bolívar's personal archivist, an unusual role for a woman to hold then. It allowed her to follow him wherever he traveled as well as to receive a paycheck from the government of Gran Colombia. Without this income, she would have been dependent on Bolívar directly for everything, a dangerous position for a woman to occupy, no matter the time.

In 1825, Bolívar began having doubts about their relationship. He wrote to her, "I see that nothing in the world can unite us under the auspices of innocence and honor." His close allies had been telling him that his ongoing affair with a married woman was too public and too scandalous. But when Sáenz hinted that she might leave him to reconcile with her husband, Bolívar couldn't take it:

> Do not go anywhere…not even with God Himself…I, too, want to see you and see you again; and touch you and smell you and taste you and unite you to me through all the senses…You are the only woman for me.

After Bolívar realized the folly of trying to end the relationship with the woman he idolized, she moved to his headquarters to be closer to him. She became a trusted member of his inner circle and was known for her loyalty, standing out even among his closest advisers and longest allies. As knowledge of their affair spread, she received petitioners who couldn't gain access to Bolívar. She acted as an intercessor for refugees, taking cases to him that she thought he might care about.

Sáenz supported Bolívar's political goals unquestioningly, even his plan to unite all South America under Gran Colombia. But his replacement of Spanish colonial power with his own made other revolutionaries unhappy. Many had fought for independent republics and now found themselves ruled by someone who wasn't that different from European powers, despite being South American by birth. Conspiracies to overthrow Bolívar developed, including one that came

Sáenz supported
Bolívar's political goals
unquestioningly, even
his plan to unite all
South America under
Gran Colombia.

from within the military on January 25, 1827. The rank and file were frustrated with Bolívar's power grab, missing wages, and a shortage of food. They seized control of the Plaza de Armas in Lima and exiled officers who were loyal to Bolívar.

Sáenz went to Lima to try to mitigate the impact of this uprising. Adopting the dress of a military colonel for herself, she gave inspiring speeches (plus wads of money) to leaders to get them to stay on Bolívar's side. She had some success and was able to smuggle out several various documents to preserve in the archive. Soon, her politicking on behalf of Bolívar earned her the nickname "La Libertadora."

Once Lima restabilized, Sáenz joined Bolívar at his personal family residence in Bogotá. He was facing issues with the people he'd long considered allies. Vice President of Gran Colombia Francisco de Paula Santander, had begun openly criticizing Bolívar's dictatorial ideas. Competing factions developed, and unrest manifested in street violence by early 1828.

Sáenz was brutally antagonistic toward Bolívar's opponents, calling them "wicked men" and praying, "God grant that [they]… die." She began collaborating with his main followers, known as the Bolivarians. The group comprised members of the country's oldest and wealthiest families, the clergy, and the army. Using a political stalemate that they had themselves manufactured, in June 1828 the Bolivarians declared the country "in crisis" and called on Bolívar to assume emergency dictatorial powers. Many moderates agreed with this proposal, seeing dictatorship as a short-term, practical measure, a "necessary evil." He accepted the call and promised to retain power only until the nation had calmed down. Reality didn't match up with his promise.

On July 28, 1828, Sáenz threw a huge party for Bolívar's birthday. It got out of control and spawned a scandal: someone made a dummy of Vice President Santander and gave it a mock trial before executing it in effigy. Some blamed this on Sáenz, saying she either had the idea or encouraged the celebrants to keep going. She denied it, but it associated her with the most extreme Bolivarians and confirmed the public's perception of her as someone with too much influence behind the scenes. People began referring to her as "la presidenta," suggesting that she was really in control, not Bolívar.

The Santanderistas, the opposition party that supported Bolívar's former vice president, was becoming a dangerous force. A couple of weeks after this scandal, on August 10, they tried to assassinate Bolívar: They planned to seize him at a theater and stab him to death. They were thwarted by Sáenz, who learned of the plot and showed up to save him.

On September 25, more conspirators sprang into action. Sixteen artillery soldiers and ten civilians broke into the presidential palace in Bogotá and made their way to Bolívar's bedroom. Astonishingly, he had been warned of this attack but dismissed it as a rumor. Instead of arranging for extra security, he relaxed and asked Sáenz to stay the night.

The two had fallen asleep by the time the conspirators broke in. She woke first, startled by his dogs barking. When she woke Bolívar, he tried to run to the door; she redirected him to the window, persuading him to escape through it into the street below. It was a narrow escape: he jumped as the attackers tried to force their way through the locked bedroom door.

When Sáenz opened the door, they grabbed her, demanding to know where Bolívar was. She told them that he was in the council room, and they forced her to lead them there. To stall them, she claimed that she didn't know where the room was. They forced her on regardless. When she stopped to take care of a wounded man, they beat her with the sides of their swords, severely injuring her. They again forced her forward, but she continued to try to help people as she went, effectively slowing down the attackers and giving Bolívar time to get away.

Finally, the attackers realized they had failed in locating Bolívar and fled. Sáenz found a doctor to take care of the people wounded inside the presidential palace then went in search of the Liberator. She found him safe but shaken. For the first time, he acknowledged that she was the *Libertadora del Libertador*.

From 1829 to 1830 Bolívar's regime grew more unstable. He resigned from the presidency on March 1, 1830, amid political tension and left Colombia in May because the tension was still rising. Sáenz stayed behind, convinced his exile was temporary. In July, she began working for his comeback by rallying local Bolivarian sentiment and cultivating sympathy within certain military battalions that guarded the presidential palace.

Sáenz was seen posting rebellious broadsides in the main square saying, "Long Live Bolívar!" On July 17, 1830, she was indicted on several charges, including "seducing" the palace guards, "insulting the public," and "dressing like a man," which "broke the rules of modesty...[and] morality." The new government wanted her exiled. She evaded the order for several weeks but eventually cooperated, retreating to Guaduas, a small town northwest of Bogotá. She may not have left out of a desire to cooperate with the government; Santanderista extremists had begun making assassination threats against her, and Bogotá was no longer safe.

In late August, Bolivarian forces overthrew the liberal Santanderista government. A group of Bogotá's powerful elite met to call for Bolívar to return from exile and resume power. At the same time, rumors sprang up that he was hopelessly ill. Sáenz refused to believe this, and in a letter to a friend she wrote, "the Liberator is immortal."

On December 17, 1830, Bolívar died, succumbing to tuberculosis that had long plagued him. After learning of his death, Sáenz postponed her plans to return to Bogotá. There's speculation about her motives. Some sources suggest she had begun to suffer from rheumatism, and her exile in a much warmer climate had soothed some of the symptoms that she was experiencing. Others suggest she was severely depressed. French scientist Jean-Baptiste Boussingault, who had long been Sáenz's friend, visited her and wrote that she had nearly died of a poisonous snake bite. She told him it had been a "science experiment," but he speculated that she had tried to imitate Cleopatra's legendary (but probably fabricated) suicide by asp bite. She eventually emerged from this darkness.

Sáenz was troubled by the direction the Bolivarian government was taking; without Bolívar, their mission had largely collapsed, and a period of partisan reprisals had begun. In 1831, Bolívar's Gran Colombia was dissolved and the Republic of New Granada formed. It covered much of the same territory but had a more republican government structure. Former Bolivarians were unhappy with this, and, because Sáenz retained her status as La Libertadora in their minds, they went to her for help planning uprisings. In 1833, Sáenz was convicted of being a part of a conspiracy to overthrow the government and on January 1, 1834, was ordered once again into exile. When she hadn't left as ordered by January 13, a group of nearly twenty soldiers, police, and convicts appeared at her door, ready to "carry her off by force."

A standoff ensued. Sáenz ordered the men to leave her property. When they didn't, she grabbed two pistols and warned that if they used force, she would not hesitate to shoot. She announced that she was tired of living and "couldn't care less about sending a few men to the next world ahead of her." Eventually, sheriff Lorenzo Lleras ordered that she be bound. She tried to fight back but was unsuccessful. The men took her to the local *divorcio*, a women's prison, and at 5:30 the next morning, soldiers led her and her servants out of Bogotá.

This unceremonious and violent banishment did not go unnoticed. US diplomat to New Granada Robert B. McAfee noted with awe, "She is as brave as Cesar as it took a guard of twenty soldiers a whole day to arrest her without killing her."[5] Local critics accused the government of going overboard, saying that denying a sick woman the chance to say goodbye to friends or receive consolation from a priest was "not something done among Christians."

Sáenz lived in impoverished exile for more than twenty years. She spent most of that time in the Peruvian port of Paita. A mix of foreign and native-born residents, including several of Sáenz's compatriots who had also been forced into exile, lived there as well. She did a little spying for various politicians but largely kept to herself; she never again politicked for change the way she had in her youth. In June 1856, Manuela Sáenz contracted a severe illness, probably diphtheria (there was an epidemic going on). She died on November 23, 1856.

After her death, she was left out of most official histories of the South American freedom movement.[6] However, thanks to the work of South American journalists, novelists, and filmmakers, her memory has been resurrected from the shadows of legend. The well-known twentieth-century Chilean poet Pablo Neruda wrote a poem to her memory titled "The Unburied Woman of Paita." Today she's seen as a feminist icon and a powerful voice for the end of slavery in South America, and the Museo Manuela Sáenz in the heart of Quito safeguards her memory.[7]

Though her blind commitment to Bolívar's dreams of South American unification seems questionable from our present, her dedication to overthrowing colonial control remains inspiring. Sáenz's life exemplifies a unique place occupied by literate upper-class women in early republican South America. Social norms dictated that women stay home to limit their contact with the "corrupting" outside world. But Manuela Sáenz found a middle ground between public and private life by using her social role to advance philosophies and plots despite being formally excluded from politics, journalism, and the military.

Tarenorerer

c. 1800 – 1831

LIKE MANY INDIGENOUS Peoples' stories, those of Tarenorerer were dismissed by the colonizers who took their homes. Large swaths of her record are lost to time. Even her name is often obscured by the name white enslavers gave her: Walyer. It's hard to say why they changed her name to this. Perhaps it meant something to them; perhaps "Tarenorerer" was too hard for British fishermen and soldiers in the early nineteenth century to pronounce.

The parts of her story that we're the surest about are the tragic parts: when and how she died. It happened in late May or early June 1831, sick in a prison after most of the rest of her tribe had been slaughtered by people who wanted to turn her homeland into sheep grazing land.

Tarenorerer was probably born in 1800. It's commonly believed that she was a member of the Tommeginne clan, which joined at least seven other clans in northwest Tasmania—a large island that is part of present-day Australia—to form the North West nation. The Tommeginne was a maritime group that relied heavily on coastal resources. While the North West clans moved up and down the coast with the seasons, the Tommeginne spent most time at Table Cape, a peninsula in northwest Tasmania.[1]

Ocher, a natural clay earth pigment, was sacred to the Tommeginne and used in both ceremonies and medicine.[2] However, there wasn't a lot of access to it in their region, so they built relationships with North nation clans to gain access. Like any political relationship, these were always in flux; the Tommeginne clan was known for using its position at Table Cape for leverage in some of these relationships. (Table Cape provided easy access to Robbins Island, which North nation clans traveled to in order to hunt and gather shells. The Tommeginne clan could deny them access if North nation clans denied access to ocher.)

Little is understood about Aboriginal spiritual beliefs or practices today because colonists didn't record much of it, but we know that each of the roughly one hundred clans had a designated animal as their

89

totem. Indigenous people called the island they lived on Trowunna, a name often forgotten.

Tarenorerer grew up in the final years of this traditional lifestyle, though no one knew that was the case then. There's little documentation of the perspective of the Aboriginal clans, but they probably knew of Europeans long before white people colonized Trowunna. Europeans had begun exploring Oceania as early as 1606, but the British were the first to establish a colony there, initially pushing Aboriginal people out of Botany Bay (now Sydney) in 1788. Only fifteen years later, in 1803, they expanded to the island of Trowunna. They called it Van Diemen's Land, for Anthony van Diemen, a governor-general of the Dutch East Indies who had funded Dutch explorer Abel Tasman's trip east. Tasman landed on the shores of Trowunna in 1642. (Colonists named the island Tasmania, after the explorer, in 1856.)

European sealers began using Van Diemen's Land as a jumping-off point for their seal hunts in the late 1700s. They established mostly transactional relationships with the local clans they encountered, trading seal carcasses, tobacco, flour, and tea for kangaroo skins. This relationship was possible precisely because sealers weren't there to stay and made no claim to the land. However, sealers were known to kidnap women from the North West nation for hunting seals and, one can guess, forced sexual relationships. At some point before 1825, Tarenorerer was one of the many women kidnapped and enslaved by sealers. She was held against her will for years, though exactly how long is unknown. During this time, she learned English and how to use a gun.

While she was enslaved, colonists came to the island to live and cleared land for their sheep to graze on. This quickly brought them into conflict with the clans that had occupied the land for generations. European observers later documented that colonists "would shoot Aborigines whenever they found them," leaving the Indigenous clans no option but to defend their homes with violence. Individual skirmishes escalated into the Black War by the mid-1820s.

Sometime in 1828, Tarenorerer escaped her enslavers. She became the leader of the Plairhekehillerplue, a clan that lived around Emu Bay, southeast of Table Cape. Her position with the Plairhekehillerplue may be where the confusion around her birth clan comes. Many clans had been decimated by colonial violence by the early 1800s, so it's likely that the Plairhekehillerplue was a collection of people from many different clans.

Tarenorerer immediately began teaching clan members to use firearms to defend themselves from the colonists and to kill the colonists' sheep and steers. She carefully instructed them to strike the colonial soldiers "when they were at their most vulnerable, between the time that their guns discharged and before they were able to reload."[3] During skirmishes with European shepherds, she would "stand on a hill and give orders to her men to attack the stockmen, taunting them to come out of their huts and be speared."

There is record that Aboriginal clans began fighting each other for limited food and power at this time. Challenged by other aspiring clan leaders, Tarenorerer escaped to Port Sorell on the northern coast with four of her siblings, some of whom the sealers had enslaved with her.

In 1829, Lieutenant Governor George Arthur hired preacher and master builder George Augustus Robinson to try to make peace between the colonists and the native people whose lands they were trying to steal. The two British officials were heavily influenced by their evangelical beliefs and the antislavery discourse sweeping the British Empire; they firmly believed that the Aboriginal Tasmanians were their "brothers in Christ" and should be saved from destruction by the colonists. But their effort toward peace was far too little and far too late; the population had already been reduced to a thousand Aborigines from an estimated six to ten thousand that had lived in Trowunna in 1803. Conflict was the main course of interaction by the time Robinson began his mission, and many people had given up hope of a peaceful solution.

Robinson kept a detailed account of his work and his concerns. He was more or less on the side of the clans who were being slaughtered. He believed that he could create peace by relocating Aborigines to missions or reservations on Swan Island, off the northeast coast of Trowunna, a trick he'd learned from the US government's treatment of Indigenous Americans. He negotiated for colonists to return land they had taken, as well as begged them to stop killing kangaroos for sport. In his journal, Robinson wrote,

> The children have witnessed the massacre of their parents and their relations carried away into captivity by these merciless invaders, their country has been taken from them, and the kangaroo, their chief subsistence, have been slaughtered wholesale for the sake of paltry lucre. Can we wonder then at the hatred they bear to the white inhabitants?...We should make some atonement for the misery we have entailed upon the original proprietors of this land.

These notes were later sent to the King William IV and published in 1966.

In his work, Robinson met Tarenorerer and recorded his thoughts about her. It's largely through Robinson that we know she existed, though his logs are seen as problematic today due to their "white savior" perspective.

On September 20, 1830, Robinson records being stalked by members of Tarenorerer's clan by the Rubicon River, near Port Sorell. He had heard of her and her warriors, who had been accused of committing violence against colonists. He wanted to capture them but thought that they intended to kill him; in the end, he didn't try. By September 30, he wrapped up this journey around Trowunna without interacting with Tarenorerer's clan.

By December 1830, Tarenorerer was captured and brought to Swan Island, where Robinson had set up reservations. She had been seized first by sealers and taken to an island in Bass Straight, the body

Tarenorerer [taught]
clan members to use firearms
to defend themselves from
the colonists and to kill
the colonists' sheep and steers.

of water separating Tasmania from Australia. She refused to work for them, then attempted to kill them while sailing with them one day. According to James Parish, a sealer who became Robinson's coxswain, Parish arrived just in time to save the sealers from Tarenorerer's revenge and single-handedly took her away. The sealers were reportedly happy to give her up, but Parish's story strains credibility. That he showed up in another ship just in time to single-handedly subdue a woman on her way to killing several sealers seems suspicious, but it's the only recorded version of the story.

Tarenorerer was not immediately identified when she arrived at Swan Island. Robinson had not met her before this moment and learned who she was only because she was "given away by her dog Whiskey and by other Aboriginal women."[4] When he realized who the sealers had captured, Robinson recorded it as a "most fortunate thing that this woman is apprehended and stopped in her murderous career....The dire atrocities she would have occasioned would be the most dreadful that can possibly be conceived."[5]

However, this wasn't the peaceful end to Tarenorerer's rebellion that Robinson hoped for. Once ensconced on a reservation on Swan Island, Tarenorerer began circulating a story that Robinson was bringing in soldiers to either jail or kill all the Indigenous people. Naturally, this caused unrest, especially because Robinson had expressly promised the people living on Swan Island that they would be safe there. Exasperated, he sent Tarenorerer away as quickly as she'd come so he could maintain order. She was forced to go with Parish while he searched for more Aboriginal women hiding in the Bass Strait Islands.

But Tarenorerer wasn't done. When she returned to Swan Island at the end of December 1830, she riled up the population within just a few hours with repeated warnings that "the white people intended shooting them." When confronted by Robinson, she told him that she "liked *lutetawin*, the white man, as much as a black snake."

By some accounts, at this point she was isolated to prevent her from inciting revolt. She was imprisoned on Gun Carriage Island, known today as Vansittart Island, where Robinson was moving the Aborigines living at his mission. Influenza and other diseases ripped through these settlements quickly, and Tarenorerer was one of their many victims. Some people note her death as May 1831, others as June 5, 1831.[6] She was probably buried in one of the graves on the island. Following what little we know about Aboriginal traditional burials, she should have either been cremated or buried in the soft sands on the beach, but probably did not receive this burial.[7]

Robinson was "relieved" when Tarenorerer died. Though many members of various clans resisted colonial oppression, he came to blame her and her soldiers for "nearly all the mischief perpetrated."[8]

The death of Tarenorerer marked the beginning of the end of the Black War. Several small groups, all that was left of the original clans of the North and North East nations, surrendered to Robinson in stages. There are no more reports of violence between colonists and Aboriginal people in the settled areas of Tasmania after January 1832. By 1835, Robinson reported that the entire Aboriginal population had been removed to various island missions and prisons that he had established. While the colonists had occasionally called for the military to "kill, destroy, and if possible, exterminate" every Aboriginal person in Tasmania, some of them did survive this war. As of 2016, more than 23,000 Tasmanians identified as Aboriginal, and Tasmanian Indigenous culture is experiencing a resurgence.[9]

All told, at least a thousand lives were lost during the Black War: about 225 colonists and anywhere from 600 to 900 Tasmanian Aboriginals. Tarenorerer was a forceful resistance fighter in a war her people ultimately lost. That so little about her is recorded is a stark reminder of how disposable the colonists saw Indigenous people in their quest for capital gain. As of 2023, discussions had begun to commission an Aboriginal artist to create a monument to the lives lost, but no memorial is currently standing.

Henry Dunant

May 8, 1828 – October 30, 1910

HENRY DUNANT IS remembered for his role in the formation of the Red Cross, one of the most recognized nongovernmental aid organizations in the world. According to his biographer, he was a sensitive soul who "wanted an immediate remedy for any unfortunate souls" he encountered.[1] However, he was also ambitious, a gambler, and prone to optimistic flights of fancy that ended up destroying his reputation during his lifetime. This duality makes him one of the most baffling but relatable people in these pages.

Jean-Henri—who later in life changed his name to Henry—Dunant was born into a bourgeois family but always aspired to wealth. Their house stood on the middle of a hillside in central Geneva, a city uniquely built to reflect economic standing: families at the top of the hill were the wealthiest and those at the bottom were day laborers. He was the oldest of six children, and his early life was idyllic. Through his mother's family, he was exposed as a child to Protestant charity, including "the young orphans" his grandfather took in.[2] Even in his youth, "something in him shook when confronted with misery and injustice."[3]

Dunant grew up during a Protestant revival in Switzerland. It became popular for upper-class young Genevan adults to gather to study the Bible, discuss theology, and pray together. After he heard Pastor François Gaussen, the famous founder of the Evangelical Society, speak in 1841 or 1842, Dunant "never recovered."[4] When he failed out of school, he became more involved with the Society. After the 1846 working-class revolution that threw out the conservative government of Geneva, he aligned himself with the aristocrats by joining the Society of Alms. For the youth of the old ruling families—and those who identified with them, like Dunant—religion was "one of the last havens for their values" and individual charity became "a kind of opposition to the state-sponsored and secular social action."[5] Dunant dedicated himself to living a life of Christian service.

In the summer of 1847, Dunant and a few friends had a deeply religious experience while hiking in the Alps. When they returned to Geneva, they started hosting meetings for Christian youth on Thursday nights. As a leader of these meetings and imbued with a mission of spreading the Gospel, Dunant began to write to aristocratic youth all over Europe, but especially in France, Germany, and England. In so doing, he began making connections that would dominate both the successes and the failures of his adulthood. Eventually, he and his friends formed Geneva chapter of the Young Men's Christian Association (YMCA).

Dunant wasn't as wealthy as his friends; he had to get a job. In 1849, he found work as a clerk at the banking house Lullin & Sauter. He didn't make much, but he donated a "remarkable" 250 francs to the Geneva YMCA.[6] With this donation, he enabled the organization to get off the ground.

Dunant's work at the bank led him into one of his most controversial missions—his entrepreneurial attempts in French-dominated Algeria. He went to oversee the bank's work there—Lullin & Sauter had been granted twenty thousand hectares of land by the prince-president of France, Louis Napoleon, nephew of the more famous Napoleon Bonaparte.[7] (In 1851, the prince-president became emperor of France and was referred to as Napoleon III.) Dunant was tasked to prepare a village for colonists in Aïn Arnat in northeast Algeria. He worked hard toward this, and he fell in love with Algeria. He began to see it not just as a beautiful place but as an ideal way for him to step into his hopes of raising his family to wealth. There's no hint that Dunant had resented his aristocratic friends for their wealth, yet in Algeria he began to dream of financial success and aristocratic greatness, which would be his downfall.

He bought a seventeen-acre plot of land near Djémila, which lies northeast of Aïn Arnat in French-controlled territory. The land had a waterfall on it "perfect for a flour mill."[8] However, he seems to have had little understanding of mills—seventeen acres would not have been enough for the equipment and livestock he would have needed to make the mill work. Dunant later sought larger land concessions and purchased bigger and riskier businesses with the hope of repairing this initial mistake. But these attempts never worked. Dunant's charm and enthusiasm meant everyone believed him whenever he came to them with a new "solution" to his business woes. In addition to risking his own money in the scheme, he risked investments from several friends and family members who supported his half-baked business ideas. They would all end up losing everything.

During a trip to Tunis in 1856–1857, Dunant wrote a travelogue of his time there, including observations on "the political system, religions, fauna and flora, the various characters, Arabic proverbs… enough to comprise a worthy document on a region of the world still quite unknown to most of Europe."[9] In it he included some humanitarian observations, including the decent treatment of enslaved people in Muslim communities when compared to the treatment in America. He spent twenty-one pages of his coverage of Tunisia condemning American slavery as "sinking deeper and deeper into the darkness of odious, inhuman and anti-Christian laws."[10]

Soon after, he wrote another booklet, *The Restoration of the Empire of Charlemagne*, a strange "'prophecy' littered with Biblical references" that attempts to trace a lineage from Charlemagne to Napoleon III as proof that the French emperor "must save Europe from anarchy."[11] Its publication date was odd timing—France had recently gone to war against Austria in favor of Italian reunification. He dedicated the book to Napoleon III, which required permission from the emperor. Seeking that permission, Dunant took a foolhardy trip through war zones to try to get this book into the hands of Napoleon III, who was commanding troops in Italy.

Dunant arrived in Italy in mid-June 1859. According to his later *Mémoires,* it was there that he met General Charles de Beaufort d'Hautpoul, who advised him not to miss the big battle happening near Solferino, Italy, in a few days. When Dunant expressed concern about the war's wounded, the general apparently said, "One does not make an omelette without breaking eggs."[12] It seems unlikely that this encounter happened exactly as Dunant relays it.[13] By other accounts the Battle of Solferino took the French by surprise, and no one expected the second War of Italian Independence to end with it. Even if Beaufort had known about the battle and its significance in advance, why would a French general tell a Swiss tourist his military plans? It's more likely that he sent Dunant north in search of General Maurice de MacMahon, who would be able to help him get his book dedication.

Dunant claims in his memoir, *A Memory of Solferino*, that he witnessed the Battle of Solferino, but he probably arrived in Castiglione on the evening of June 24, after the brutal fighting had ended. French and Austrian troops and wounded soldiers were staggering into the three cities closest to the battleground, Castiglione among them, as he appeared. At least thirty-seven thousand people had fallen in a single day of combat, and the spectacle of them overwhelmed Dunant.[14]

Though everyone knew the battle was going on, no one had prepared to deal with its aftermath. Castiglione became "a vast improvised hospital," but treatment was not going well there.[15] The city government opened churches, homes, and government buildings to the wounded, but still hundreds of wounded soldiers bled out in the streets of Castiglione while still others died slowly on the battlefield, unable to stumble elsewhere for help. In *A Memory of Solferino*, Dunant wrote,

> The stillness of the night was broken by groans, by stifled sighs of anguish and suffering. Heart-rending voices kept calling for help. Who could ever describe the agonies of that fearful night![16]

Horrified by what he saw, Dunant sprang into action. He spent the night and the next day tending to wounded soldiers, "giving fresh water to parched lips, writing down a goodbye, comforting a last breath, relieving those he could, without plan or method."[17] He worked like a "solitary aid worker," overwhelmed and undersupplied.[18]

He must have quickly felt a sense of frustration. There weren't enough medical supplies, and no one was organizing a way of acquiring more. There was enough water, but soldiers left alone in the sun were dying of thirst. Civilian women were available to help, but they had no training.

In her biography of Dunant, Corinne Chaponnière supposes he probably didn't sleep well that night—not just because of the horrors of war, however:

> It wasn't just the unacceptable waste of so many lives lost or ruined on a single Saturday in June; the lives of young men who were nearly his own age, who could have been his brothers or his cousins. No, what truly haunted him that night was the confusion, the disorganization, the frantic *improvisation* of a city that had known a battle was looming, had even hoped for Allied liberation, and yet was totally unprepared when it arrived. How many extra lives had this cost? Was it inevitable that war continued to kill even days after a battle had ended?[19]

Something had to be done.

On June 26, 1859, Dunant, seeing that no one else was going to, began organizing. He engaged young boys to ferry water and women to dress wounds. He freed Austrian doctors from jail and put them to work. He sent his personal coachman to nearby towns to purchase whatever supplies he could find: bandages, sponges, herbs, food, tobacco, and clothing.[20] Other tourists and journalists were passing through, so he put them to work, giving them tasks "as long as they could bear it."[21] Dunant gave immense credit to the women of the town: "All honour to these compassionate women, to these girls of Castiglione! Imperturbable, unwearying, unfaltering, their quiet self-sacrifice made little of fatigue and horrors, and of their own devotion."[22] He set the standard that each soldier should be treated the same, regardless of their nationality or the side they had fought on.

This was a revolutionary concept—usually armies treated only their own soldiers, leaving other wounded to die or heal alone.

About eighteen months after the battle, Dunant collected his memories of the battle's gruesome aftermath in *A Memory of Solferino*, a book that described the grisly violence of war so vividly it still turns stomachs. From reading *Uncle Tom's Cabin*, he had learned that "beliefs are born of emotions."[23] He knew that minute descriptions of the horrors he had witnessed would inspire an emotional response similar to that of Harriet Beecher Stowe's novel, which was exactly what he wanted. Nevertheless, Dunant was careful to remain impartial in his coverage, honoring the bravery and suffering of both sides. His book was a sensation.

Once he finished his account of Solferino, Dunant posed a radical question: "Would it not be possible, in times of peace and quiet, to form relief societies for the purpose of having care given to the wounded in wartime by zealous, devoted and thoroughly qualified volunteers?"[24]

Realizing that he had come up with an important idea, Dunant pushed forward, targeting high-ranking government officials and nobles, trying to get people in power to agree to an international group of volunteer medical professionals who would be treated as neutral in any war zone. Every part of his suggestion was unheard of—relief societies sprang up and faded away; medical professionals were members of the military and subject to being treated as such; working together to make war less devastating undercut the point of war in the first place. Initially, the idea received a lot of pushback, including from Florence Nightingale, the mother of modern nursing who had advocated for better medical education for women after treating soldiers during the Crimean War.[25]

Dunant helped form a committee of five people to develop his idea into a real proposal that could be presented at a welfare conference in Berlin. When the conference was canceled, the committee members decided to simply host their own conference in Geneva, despite having met only three times in six months.[26] They invited the governments of Europe to send delegates, and many did. Austria, Bavaria, Spain, France, Great Britain, the Netherlands, Sweden, Italy, and Russia, among others, were all represented.

By the time of the October 1863 conference, however, Dunant had upset the other four people on his committee. Without consulting them, he had added aid-worker neutrality to the public list of goals. Neutrality in war was not a familiar concept to governments at this time, and Dunant's earlier proposals had only mentioned international cooperation for the establishment of international aid-workers. Designating medical personnel as neutral made them off limits for attack; Dunant's committee members probably worried that this would be too radical for some governments, who might see not being allowed to attack a hospital both as an encroachment on their sovereignty and as a tactical loss. Dunant was unapologetic for this oversight, and the other committee members punished him by not allowing him to speak at his own conference.[27]

Nevertheless, the initial conference accomplished all of Dunant's goals. Together the delegates created ten resolutions, including aid-worker neutrality, and three "wishes" for an international relief committee. The Genevan organizing committee had thrown around the idea of a symbol all aid-workers could wear since its earliest discussions, but it was member Dr. Louis Appia who proposed that a white band worn on the left arm be made standard.

The red cross was added "after some discussion," but who suggested it isn't extant in the minutes of the meeting, nor explicitly credited to anyone, which means we don't know who created one of the single most recognizable symbols on Earth.[28] Though the red cross looks like an inversion of the Swiss national flag, we don't know if the visual reference to Switzerland was deliberate. The Swiss national flag had been adopted fewer than twenty years before the conference, but a white cross on a red background had been the insignia of Swiss soldiers since the fourteenth century. It seems like a link between the red cross and the Swiss flag is there, but we may never have confirmation.[29]

Of course, this conference was not binding, it was just a collection of ideas. Next up was creating and signing an international treaty, then ratifying it.

Just ten months after the meeting, in August 1864, sixteen countries—including Brazil, the United States, and Portugal, who had all been missing from the first conference—sent twenty-six delegates to Geneva to hammer out the treaty. Today we know this meeting as the First Geneva Convention, which radically altered the way nations treat wounded and sick soldiers. Three more conventions followed in the next century, expanding the original mission to include maritime warfare, prisoners of war, and civilians. The International Committee of the Red Cross is still dedicated to enforcing the treaties as a basis of international humanitarian law.

Dunant's life after the creation of the Red Cross was rocky. His speculations in Algeria didn't pan out, and, worse, he was accused of deliberately swindling various people and banks. He was kicked off the committee for the Red Cross, and the Geneva YMCA distanced itself from him publicly. Bankrupt and hated in Geneva, he fled to France in May 1867; he never returned home.[30] Gustave Moynier, president of the committee that created the Red Cross, so hated his former colleague that he went out of his way to block aid to Dunant for years after, ensuring that Dunant was forced to live in poverty and squalor in Paris. For a long time, Dunant was mostly forgotten while the Red Cross continued without him.

Around 1893, Dunant became an advocate for women's rights. Gender equality, which was linked with the republicanism he'd hated in his youth, was a surprising ideal for him to champion.[31] Too old to agitate himself, he mentored a young French activist, Sara Bourcart, by letter.[32]

His attraction to gender equality led him into the female-dominated pacifist camp, and in 1895 he befriended Baroness Bertha von Suttner, author of the influential antiwar novel *Lay Down Your Arms!* When she learned that the Red Cross had pushed Dunant out, she began lobbying her friend Alfred Nobel to endow a financial grant that could be used by determined and accomplished people like Dunant to further peace. Little did she know, Nobel had already sketched out plans to use his wealth for just such a grant in his will. After Nobel died in December 1896, the terms of his will were revealed, and the Nobel Prize—including the Nobel Peace Prize—created.

On December 10, 1901, Henry Dunant was among the first two recipients of the Nobel Peace Prize for his work establishing the Red Cross.[33] Thus redeemed from obscurity, he began to have awards heaped on him from all corners. Yet he never used award money to pay off his debts or even move into nicer lodgings. He died in 1910, still in the basic hospice room he'd occupied since 1892.[34] In his will, he donated about thirteen thousand francs to keep a bed open at his nursing home in Heiden, Switzerland, for impoverished local people. He donated the rest of his money to various philanthropic organizations.

In an 1890 letter, Dunant claimed he wanted to be "buried in the ground like a dog."[35] His family didn't follow these instructions to the letter, but they did cremate him and laid his ashes to rest in Zurich without any fanfare.

Sun Yat-sen

November 12, 1866 – March 12, 1925

EIGHT HUNDRED YEARS after Huang Chao (page 20) brought about the demise of the Tang dynasty, another strong dynasty rose in China: the Qing dynasty, sometimes called the Manchu dynasty. Its leaders were outsiders, invaders from Manchuria who had taken over the capital in Beijing and ruled over the Han Chinese people who made up the majority of the population. Initially, the Qing era had been another golden era of Chinese history: 150 years of stability and prosperity. In the late eighteenth century, China was "easily the most extensive, populous, powerful, and prosperous" country on Earth.[1] But by the end of the nineteenth century, the empire was in decline and facing threats from a much more modern outside world. Unhappy with how China had fallen behind, dissidents began to rise.

Sun Yat-sen was one of these dissidents. He was born in 1866 to a family of impoverished farmers. The Sun family lived in Cuiheng, a small village in Guangdong Province, one of the most troubled regions of China at the time. Geographically isolated from the capital of Beijing, it had an unchecked opium trade that devastated the population; the area became fertile ground for secret societies that raised rebels and rebellions. The confluent challenges of opium, poverty, and overpopulation fueled a desperation that the Qing dynasty couldn't fix with moderate reforms.

One of four surviving children, Sun had a hardscrabble early life. His family owned a plot of land too small to support it, and Sun's mother had her feet bound, restricting her ability to contribute to household income. Sun rarely reflected on his early life, though, so little is known about it. He probably attended elementary school and helped his father work their land.

In 1879, his older brother Sun Mei paid for Sun to join him in Honolulu. There, Sun Yat-sen attended 'Iolani School, an Anglican missionary institution and bastion of anti-Americanism. Hawaii was an independent nation at the time, and teachers at the 'Iolani School championed Hawaiian independence against American annexation.

Sun biographer Tjio Kayloe supposes that this early exposure to rhet-orics of independence planted the seeds for Sun's anti-imperialism and sensitivity to Western aggression later in his life.

After graduating from 'Iolani, Sun attended the prestigious Oahu School. Both schools were heavily influenced by Protestant mission-aries, and he found himself drawn to Christianity. His conversion infuriated Sun Mei, who saw it as betrayal of their ancestors, and his brother sent Sun Yat-sen back to China in 1883 to "take this Jesus nonsense out of him." Instead of forcing him to abandon his faith, Sun's father allowed him to move to Christian-friendly Hong Kong to study medicine—the only professional option open to him in China without a degree. He was baptized by an American missionary in Hong Kong that fall. In 1884, Sun married Lu Muzhen in an arranged marriage. The couple had a son and two daughters.

Living in English-controlled Hong Kong, Sun began to see flaws in Chinese society. China, once a leader of innovation, had fallen behind its neighbors like Japan and Russia. Furthermore, Western powers like France and England were increasingly carving up China's territory for their own commercial use. Sun befriended several stu-dents whose anti-Manchu sentiments reflected his own, and through them he learned about the secret societies of Guangdong, the main-land province adjacent to Hong Kong. Some of the societies had a centuries-long avowed mission to overthrow the Qing dynasty and restore the Han Chinese Ming dynasty, and Sun realized the revolu-tionary power of these groups. They would play a major role in his later revolutionary plans.

Considering his dual beliefs in Christianity and revolution, it's unsurprising that Sun was a fan of the Taiping Rebellion. The Taiping forces were a "cult-like group" who tried to overthrow the Qing dynasty over economic conditions; their philosophy was based in Christian ideas. They severely weakened the Qing dynasty during their rebellion from 1850 to 1864 but were ultimately unsuccessful. When Sun began experimenting with building bombs in medical school, his friends affectionately called him "Hong Xiuquan" after the Taiping founder. Sun began reading, in addition to texts on the Taiping Rebellion, the major Western philosophers like Jean-Jacques Rousseau and John Stuart Mill and incorporating their political beliefs into his own.

After medical school, Sun opened the Chinese Western Apothecary in Macau. But by 1894, his dissatisfaction with the Qing regime took center stage. He closed his business and returned to Hawaii that fall to begin his life as a professional rebel, setting sail amid a raging war between China and Japan.

While he'd been in Hong Kong, his brother Sun Mei had become rather wealthy on the island of Maui. At some point, he took in Sun Yat-sen's wife and children and financially supported them, as well as bankrolled many of Sun's rebellious schemes. With his brother's support, Sun began reaching out to many *huaqiao*, Chinese citizens living abroad, seeking support for a revolution. Few were initially interested, however. Confucian values meant that a whole family was responsible when one member committed a crime; huaqiao feared reprisals against family members in China if their involvement with a revolutionary was discovered. Sun eventually convinced a small group to form the Revive China Society, described by French historian Marie-Claire Bergère as "a group of conspirators linked by...their shared dissatisfaction with the established order. It was less concerned with politics...than with immediate action."[2]

Sun had his first shot at revolution in October 1895. He returned to Hong Kong with members of Revive China, intending to capture Guangdong and Guangxi while China reeled after a disastrous military loss to Japan. Sun hoped that the fall of the two provinces would serve as inspiration for other secret societies inclined toward revolution to rise up and move toward Beijing itself. Though their plans were detailed and they recruited a strike force of a few thousand, their scheme fell apart almost immediately. Police captured the would-be rebels as they sailed from Hong Kong; several were executed and Sun only "narrowly" escaped. He fled to Japan, beginning a sixteen-year exile from China.

Japan became something of a home base for Sun for a while. Biographer Tjio supposes that though some people were hesitant to be seen consorting with "a terrorist with a price on his head," Sun's attempted coup made him popular particularly among Chinese students studying abroad in Japan. He'd had surprisingly little traction with young intellectuals before this point. It would take Sun a long time to warm up to the students, but he eventually realized that this rising intelligentsia lent his goals a patina of respectability that he'd been missing by relying on only criminal secret societies. The students, meanwhile, were attracted to Sun's unparalleled knowledge of the West after years spent abroad.

His absence from China didn't mean that Sun quit trying to free Chinese citizens from bad government. Sun would be "instrumental in at least ten abortive rebellions" over the years; their failures made him increasingly famous and also increasingly frustrated.[3] Sun became a figurehead for the Chinese revolution, which ended his financial troubles. As his fame and popularity grew, however, foreign governments became uncomfortable hosting him. By 1907, even Japan, which had been secretly supporting Sun to further its own aspirations of taking over China, asked Sun to leave (though the government gave him a large sum of money to help him on his way).[4]

During his exile, he was caught once—in 1896 in London. He was detained for thirteen days inside the Chinese Legation until British pressure and public rallying embarrassed the Chinese into releasing him. He spent much of the rest of his exile touring the United States and Europe, trying to rally support from the Chinese diaspora and foreign powers. However, supporters were split between Sun with his republican aims and others who wanted to replace the Manchus with a different emperor, preserving the monarchical structure.

This exile gave Sun time to cut his teeth on political philosophy. He had never been formally educated in political science;

consequently, many of his early ideas were naive or not fully formed. In 1897 he was introduced to pan-Asianism by Minakata Kumagusu, a Japanese botanist living in England. He confided in Sun his fervent hope that Asians would drive all Westerners out of Asia and unite under one political and economic structure; the idea inspired the rest of Sun's philosophy.

By 1905, Sun crystallized his Three Principles of the People philosophy. Inspired by Abraham Lincoln's phrase "Government of the people, by the people, for the people," Sun called for *"minzu, minquan, minsheng,"* usually translated as a people's nation, a people's franchise, and a people's life.[5] With this slogan, he proposed a five-branch government loosely based on the American system. It would have an executive, legislative, and judicial branch, like the us system, but would add an examination branch to continue screening candidates for government positions and a censorate branch to check up on the other four branches.

In the early twentieth century, Sun became the central figure around which an alliance of dissent groups orbited. They were attracted to his long personal history of dedication to revolution, his international connections, and the force of his personality—he was often noted as having a "gentlemanly demeanor." Everyone connected with Sun agreed that it was time for the Qing dynasty to go—what would happen next was more contentious. Eventually, he had supporters in several countries, including Singapore, New Zealand, the us, and South Africa. Despite the increased support, Sun wasn't hopeful that the revolution would begin soon.

But then, help came from a surprising place: the Qing dynasty. For ten years the Empress Dowager Cixi had been allowing moderate reforms, including reorganizing the army. But the empress had little control over these parts of the military, called the New Army. In fact, many of its members were joining anti-dynastic societies and using their military connections to plan a revolution.

Inspired by
Abraham Lincoln's phrase
"Government of the people,
by the people, for the people,"
Sun called for "*minzu,
minquan, minsheng*," usually
translated as a people's
nation, a people's franchise,
and a people's life.

On October 9, 1911, a group of revolutionaries in Wuhan, Hubei Province, accidentally detonated a bomb. In the ensuing investigation, police discovered the names of several New Army soldiers on a roster of insurgents. Tensions escalated quickly, and the next evening Sergeant Xiong Bingkun of the Eighth Engineer Battalion persuaded his men to mutiny. Together they seized an armory and attacked Wuhan's fort, scaring the Qing-loyal governor-general into abandoning the city; the New Army took over in a single night. Their success at Wuhan inspired revolutionaries to capture the city of Hanyang the next day, and then Hankou a day later. By the end of the month, six cities and provinces had revolted. The Chinese Revolution had begun.

Sun read about the revolution in the newspaper on October 11. He was in Denver, Colorado, at the time, raising money to support his efforts. Probably realizing that the revolutionary movement would need money more than ever (and that people might be more likely to give to a cause with a success record), Sun remained on his tour, proceeding to Chicago. En route, he picked up a newspaper that reported that he would be the first president of the republic if the revolution succeeded—it was the first he'd heard about it.

On the cusp of his twenty-year-long dream coming true, Sun did not immediately return to China. Tjio supposes that he would have been concerned for his own safety. After all, at this point, only Hubei Province has successfully overturned local Qing power. If the revolution failed, Sun would be walking into a certain death sentence. According to his memoir, Sun proceeded instead to Washington, D.C., to ensure foreign neutrality: "Our diplomatic front was more important even than the military front."[6] Then he went to England, hoping that if that country took his side, Japan would follow suit.[7] There he met up with his wife and children, who, it seems, he hadn't seen in years.

While he had been contacting foreign governments, revolutionaries had continued to rise up—by December, they controlled sixteen provinces, including areas within striking distance of the Qing capital at Beijing. In late November, Sun set sail for China for the first time in sixteen years. He was accompanied by his wife, children, and a few close Chinese comrades.

He landed in Shanghai on December 25. It quickly became clear that the report that he would be president had been premature — instead, a jockeying for power was taking place between several politicians: Yuan Shikai, Huang Xing, and Li Yuanhong. According to Bergère, "Nobody had even considered making Sun Yat-Sen head of state" before this moment.[8] But they immediately saw the usefulness of making him president provisionally — as the face of the revolutionary alliance, he could symbolically "confirm the political standing of the South and China's entry into the republican era."[9] Once he was confirmed, the country was still in an awkward position — Sun was provisional president, based in Nanjing (China's historic capital) while the emperor still sat on the throne in Beijing.

Yuan Shikai, provisional prime minister of the new government, had wanted the presidency for himself. Placed in charge of negotiating with the Qing dynasty for its abdication, he suddenly dug in his heels, rejecting the agreement he'd helped hammer out. Stuck at an impasse, Sun was forced to promise to make Yuan president if he could get the Qing to abdicate peacefully. To ensure his compatriots would stick to the promise, Yuan snuck a clause into the Qing abdication edict that gave the power to form a provisional republican government to himself alone. The rest of the revolutionaries — along with the rest of China — were "incensed" when they read it but were stuck with it.

On February 14, 1912, after just forty-five days as the provisional president, Sun Yat-sen resigned the presidency. He proceeded to the tomb of the Hongwu Emperor, founder of the Ming dynasty, and announced to the spirit that the Manchu conquest of Ming China had finally been avenged.

If Sun was disappointed by this turn of events, he didn't explicitly say so. In an article in *The Strand Magazine* the next month, he wrote,

I have done my work; the wave of enlightenment and progress cannot now be stayed and China—the country in the world most fitted to be a republic, because of the industrious and docile character of the people—will, in a short time, take her place amongst the civilized and liberty-loving nations of the world.[10]

Despite this hopeful tone, Sun spent the rest of his life fighting an unstable government's tendency toward warlordism. A series of aborted revolutionary movements sprang up in the following years, occasionally with Sun at the center. Yuan quickly fell from grace and, a decade later, the new Soviet government began courting Sun, influencing him to reorganize the Nationalist Party on the Soviet model. In 1925, Sun suddenly died of cancer.

Ultimately, Sun's goal of transforming China into a republic free of foreign influence failed. Although he is often sanctified by followers and is remembered as a pioneer of the Chinese Revolution, his work is seen by some as unfinished.

Mary Moloney

September 29, 1878 – December 1, 1921

MARY MOLONEY WAS born in Sandycove, Dublin, Ireland, to Edward O'Connor and Crosdella Moloney. Not much is known about her early life, nor her adult life. But for a brief moment during Winston Churchill's early career, she became famous for her unique style of protest.

At birth, her full name was Horatia Dorothy Moloney O'Connor. Her surname is alternately spelled Molony and Maloney, but Moloney is the surname listed for her mother in the Glasthule Parish Records.[1] She began using her mother's maiden name at some point, dropping O'Connor. Her given name is alternately listed as Dolly, a common nickname for Dorothy. But in many records, she's listed simply as "Miss Moloney," even when other women's first names are listed.

We don't know when Moloney joined the fight for women's suffrage. As she was born in 1878, we can guess the mid to late 1890s. By that point, the battle for women's voting rights in the United Kingdom had been going on for more than two hundred years. Precious little progress had been made during that time; even Queen Victoria ably ruling the country didn't seem to have an impact. The reality was that women were still considered the property of their husbands or fathers in England.

The middle of the nineteenth century had seen passage of the Custody of Infants Act, which allowed women access to their children after divorce. John Stuart Mill, a towering intellectual of the time, had spoken publicly in defense of equality for women, though not much came of his philosophy until he was elected to Parliament in 1865. Even then, his attempt to substitute "person" in place of "man" in the Reform Bill was unsuccessful.[2]

The call for votes for women accelerated throughout the nineteenth century. Societies for women's suffrage popped up around the UK; often several existed in a single city. The historical narrative of this movement has long focused on the efforts of white upper-class women, making it seem that middle-class women, working-class women, and women of color were content to not vote. But as historian Amanda Vickery points out in the documentary *Suffragettes Forever!*, the 1851 birth of the Sheffield Female Political Association disputes that. It was an organization of middle-class women working for women's suffrage after their support of the Chartists goal for universal male voting rights had gone unappreciated.

On October 10, 1903, Emmeline Pankhurst and her daughters Christabel and Sylvia founded the Women's Social and Political Union (WSPU) in England. She and her family had previously been active in the Independent Labour Party but felt that the party no longer represented their interests. WSPU was open only to women and had no political affiliation; instead, its mission was to attack whichever political party was in power until it introduced legislation that included enfranchisement. Its members became known for splashy protests, like following ministers to their country homes to protest. The group swelled quickly. It's possible that Moloney joined WSPU during this time, though without the group's membership lists, this can't be confirmed.

In 1906, an envoy representing three hundred women and several different suffrage groups gained a meeting with Prime Minister Sir Henry Campbell-Bannerman. They laid out an argument to him that he called "conclusive and irrefutable."[3] Nevertheless, he "proposed to do nothing at all about it" and encouraged the women to "go on pestering" the government and remain patient.[4] It was a galling thing for the women to be told to remain patient when they had already been waiting for generations.

Within WSPU, tensions had already reached a boiling point. This unsuccessful meeting caused the Pankhurst women running the WSPU to rethink their strategy. The women were getting palpably frustrated with the lack of progress. In their eyes, years of peaceful demonstration and appeals to reason hadn't worked, so a new strategy was needed.

The era of revolt began.

By this point, women had realized the unique power of getting arrested. Each trial allowed them to say something in their defense—a unique chance to speak in front of the men who could influence law. The *Illustrated London News* reported on arrests of suffragists, spreading their message further. Each trial became a platform. Lists of arrestees after a protest became known as the "roll of honour" for each occasion.[5] In marches, women who had been imprisoned wore white, a color of honor.[6] Today, white remains a symbolic color for the women's movement as a nod to these early activists.

In 1907, Christabel Pankhurst, the daughter of Emmeline Pankhurst, announced that future WSPU decisions would be made by a committee she appointed. Over seventy women disagreed with this decision and left to form the competing Women's Freedom League (WFL), a more democratic association. Moloney became an organizer for the league, and under its banner led the protest that made her famous: refusing to let Winston Churchill speak.

On Tuesday, May 5, 1908, the *Irish Times* reported on her actions in Dundee, Scotland under the headlines "Amusing Scenes" and "Mr. Churchill and the Suffragettes."[7] The day before, Moloney had interrupted Churchill's campaign stop. He had been scheduled to speak to workers outside the Blackness Foundry as part of his bid to be reelected to Parliament.

Before Churchill arrived, Moloney and her supporters set up camp in front of the workers, who had arrived early to get a good spot to see Churchill. Moloney gave a speech of her own. She "complained of a passage in a speech [Churchill] delivered," in which he claimed that the suffragettes were "allying themselves with the forces of drink and reaction. They were carried shoulder-high...by the rowdy elements, which are always to be found at a publichouse-made manifestation."[8] His words were an attempt to disgrace the women by implying they had loose morals; this was one of the many ways people opposed to women's equality tried to discredit the suffrage movement. Moloney saw the words as slander.

Moloney not only argued against Churchill but also demanded a public apology for the insult. "Until Mr. Churchill apologizes for an infamous insult he has offered to the women, as far as I and my friends are concerned, he shall not get a hearing anywhere in Dundee."[9] She added that she was not carried in any man's arms, presumably as a statement of her own independence. When a man in the crowd heckled her by saying, "I suppose you would like to be, though," Moloney threatened that, "if any man attempted to lift her in his arms she would have boxed his ears."[10] There are no reports of anyone trying, so we can assume Moloney was safe from the crowd.

By the time Churchill arrived, the crowd of five or six hundred was "in full possession of the ladies."[11] More disconcerting to him, these working-class men seemed to agree with the WFL: he received a "rather tepid reception" as he took the stage.[12]

Perhaps Churchill sensed that this was not going to be a comfortable campaign stop, because he quickly reentered his vehicle and seemed to be about to speak from it when he was interrupted. A carriage pulled up next to his car, and from inside of it leaned Mary Moloney, ringing a huge bell.

For the next several minutes, every time Churchill tried to speak, Moloney clanged her bell. She created "so much din that the voice of [Churchill] could not be heard more than a few yards away."[13] Amused by her, some of the crowd joined in her disruption and began jeering at Churchill.

Churchill and his chauffeur tried to move his car to escape Moloney's interruptions. But she quickly gave chase in her carriage, once again leaning out her window to clang her bell until Churchill couldn't be heard.

Again, Churchill tried to move, but the carriage followed, with Moloney ringing her bell. At this point, Churchill sat down and lit a cigarette to pass some time, apparently "intending to tire the ladies out."[14] Moloney used the opportunity to demand an apology from him in front of the crowd. "Who is the strongest—an Irish woman or Mr. Winston Churchill?" She heckled him.[15]

At this point Churchill gave up and left after petulantly saying,

Observe the regard they have for freedom of speech. Let her ring her bell. If she thinks that a reasonable and serious argument to use in Dundee, I don't care. It, at any rate, saves me the trouble of making a speech.[16]

When he left, the women tried to follow in their carriage, but the crowd had had enough. They seized the horses by their bridles, keeping them from following Churchill. For the night, at least, Churchill got away. It's unclear whether Moloney had a particular grudge against Churchill for the way he talked about women or if she had been assigned by the larger WFL chapter to protest his campaign stops while other members protested other candidates. Regardless, many reports say that Moloney continued to drown out his campaign speeches in Dundee for a full week. Nevertheless, he won the by-election and returned to Parliament. He went on to become prime minister in 1940.

According to Sylvia Pankhurst, daughter of WSPU founder Emmeline, Moloney's bell-ringing exploits earned her the nickname "La Belle Maloney" in suffrage circles. It was a dual reference to her beauty and the bell she used to interrupt Churchill.

Several months later, Moloney was part of a troop of women who entered the House of Commons in London while it was in session. Over a dozen members of WFL sat in the upper-story Ladies' Gallery in St. Stephen's Hall, often nicknamed the Ladies' Cage due to the metal grilles over the windows.[17] They were "young, well dressed in tailor-made costumes, and by their behavior appeared to indicate they were entirely unknown to each other."[18] At 8:30 a.m. on the dot, two of the women chained themselves to the iron grill that separated the women's gallery from the rest of the chamber.

Chaos erupted. While the women were unchained from the grilles, Moloney led three other women in an attempt to get into the House of Lords to speak and throw down pamphlets. They found the door locked, so they climbed atop the Richard I sculpture opposite the entrance to the chamber. From the plinth several feet in the air, Moloney began to give her speech. She and three of her coconspirators eluded capture for a while, giving their speech to a growing crowd, but eventually they were dragged down by police and arrested. Twelve women in total were arrested that day. Someone paid Moloney's bail, "much to her chagrin."[19]

At this point in the history of the struggle for women's suffrage, a distinction developed between suffragists and suffragettes. Suffragists campaigned for the women's vote peacefully, while suffragettes turned to increasingly aggressive means as the campaign dragged into the twentieth century. Their mission statement was "deeds not words," and they were happy to be confrontational in their mission.[20] They followed members of Parliament to their private homes, lit arson, and set bombs in public spaces to get their message across. The WSPU defended these actions by pointing out that over a century of suffragists' peaceful work had achieved nothing.[21] As a result of their increased militancy, over a thousand suffragettes were arrested and incarcerated at Holloway Prison in London between 1906 and 1913.

For these women, it was important that they be treated as political prisoners instead of criminals. To reinforce this, hundreds of suffragettes went on hunger strikes, a tactic embedded in Irish and UK political tradition.[22] The government responded with brutal forced feedings, some of which killed the women they tried to treat. When the brutality of this practice made the government look bad, they began releasing from prison suffragettes who were getting weak from their hunger strikes. Once the women were well enough to protest in public again, they were arrested again; the practice became known as the Cat and Mouse Act.[23]

Moloney was, strictly speaking, a suffragist. Her bell-ringing protest and trespassing at Parliament were excellent stunts, but they were still nonviolent compared to the actions of the suffragettes. In the documentary series *Suffragettes Forever!*, historian Fern Riddell compared the efforts of the WSPU to terrorist strategies. They targeted national communication lines and incited some fear among the British population around going to everyday places like church or the theater. In June 1914, suffragettes planted a bomb in Westminster Abbey, damaging the coronation chair but not hurting anyone.[24]

When World War I disrupted Europe, most suffragist societies suspended campaigning for the vote. They used their organizing powers to support the war instead. In 1918, Parliament passed an act granting the vote to all women over the age of thirty who owned property or were married to someone who did.[25]

History mostly lost track of Moloney after her arrest for climbing the sculpture of Richard I. She may have been present at the infamous Black Friday protests in November 1910, when three hundred members of the WSPU marched to the Houses of Parliament and were violently attacked by over one thousand male police officers and several dozen civilian men. The attacks lasted for six hours and included sexual assault. They resulted in the deaths of two women. Winston Churchill, by then the home secretary, tried to suppress the full story of what happened that day from getting out, but newspapers like *Votes for Women* printed accounts of the protest. When the horror of the testimony was finally made public, it encouraged support for suffrage from people who had otherwise been ambivalent.[26]

In 1911, Moloney married Egbert T. Lancaster, when she was thirty-three years old. Together they had a daughter. It seems that she might have stopped pursuing activism once she settled into the routines of marriage and motherhood. She died in December 1921, soon after giving birth to a son at forty-three years old. She was remembered by other members of the Women's Freedom League. In their obituary of her for *The Vote* newspaper, they described her as, "Dolly Malony, the bright and bonny and resourceful little Irish girl, who rang the bell at Mr. Churchill's historic Dundee election, when the women decided he should not be allowed to speak."[27]

Amelio Robles Ávila

November 3, 1889 – December 9, 1984

THE MEXICAN REVOLUTION (1910–20) made room for more than just a new national government in Mexico; for many, it created room to take on new identities and forge new futures for themselves. Amelio Robles Ávila was one of those people.

One of the earliest recorded transgender figures in Latin America, Robles was assigned female when he was born on November 3, 1889.[1] Growing up in Xochipala, rural Guerrero, at the turn of the twentieth century, Amelio came from a family of ranchers. They were midsize landowners, and when the Mexican Revolution swept through, they, like similar families, took center stage.

Amelio's father, Casimiro Robles, died when Amelio was young. His mother, Josefa Ávila, remarried, but Amelio apparently never got along with his stepfather.[2] He had several siblings and half-siblings, many of whom he remained close to his entire life. As landowners, most of the family never moved out of Xochipala.

Probably as a preteen, Robles joined the Daughters of María, a Catholic group "dedicated to refining young women's spiritual education."[3] This meant that the nuns taught the girls traditional female tasks, like cooking and cleaning, in addition to overseeing their religious studies. By some accounts, Robles had a rebellious nature even as a teen, which couldn't be tamed even by the nuns he saw daily.[4] Around this time, Robles "courted a schoolmate as her beau." Though Robles still dressed in traditionally feminine clothing at this point, he generally took on the "masculine" role in romantic relationships, mimicking heteronormative expectations for relationship roles. That included pursuing and seducing the schoolmate he was interested in.

As was expected, Robles worked in the family restaurant, which served food to revolutionaries passing through the area during the early stages of the revolution. He also learned how to handle weapons and became adept at riding horses. His prowess with a firearm atop a horse was seen as a "good spectacle" in his hometown. As a youth, Robles wanted to grow up to be a doctor, a traditionally masculine profession.

In 1910, dictator Porfirio Díaz won another term as president in a sham election. Díaz had handpicked aristocratic Francisco Madero to run against him, knowing he would lose. However, Díaz had not expected Madero to become popular enough to successfully lead a military revolution against him.

After the election, Madero had temporarily fled to Texas, proclaimed himself president of Mexico, and reentered Mexico, collecting groups of peasant guerrilla forces with him as he traveled south. One of these groups was the Liberation Army of the South, led by Emiliano Zapata. Zapata had a history of forcefully winning power and land for the oft-ignored mestizo and Indigenous people in the state of Morelos, in south central Mexico, and had emerged as a leader and voice for the people.

Zapata's forces defeated Díaz's army in the Battle of Cuautla in May 1911. Díaz later admitted that the fall of Cuautla convinced him to resign. The Mexican government, deeply in debt and unpopular, collapsed, and Díaz retreated into exile in May 1911.

October 1911 saw Madero formally elected to office. But by November, it was clear that the inexperienced leader didn't know what he was doing. Frustrated by what he saw as Madero's betrayed promises, Zapata wrote and published the Plan of Ayala in late November, which called for land reform and denounced Madero's presidency.[5] It effectively united smaller rebellions and general discontent under the goal of redistributing land that had been bought up and stolen by wealthy landowners and consolidated into large haciendas.

Under this call, Robles joined Zapata's Liberation Army in 1912 or 1913. According to historian Gabriela Cano, Robles's inspiration might have been less about the agrarian cause than about "passion for the intensity of war, so full of dangers and strong emotions." Later in life, when reminiscing about the revolution, Robles said little about agrarianism and politics and more about the daily life of the battlefield and exploits with comrades.

Though Robles had always preferred masculine hobbies, it's unclear when he began wearing masculine fashion and asking that people use masculine pronouns to refer to him. Possibly it began in 1911 or so, when many women began adopting masculine clothing for safety. War zones are often sites of sexual violence against the female population, and effectively disguising oneself as a man could go a long way to avoiding this inhumanity.

However, the women in Mexico who adopted male disguise for their safety or to fight in the revolution usually removed their disguise once the war was over. (Women who fought in Zapata's army include Colonel Juana Gutiérrez de Mendoza, who lobbied Zapata to stop the abuse soldiers perpetrated on women.) Beginning his transition might have been easier in such a historic moment, but it's clear from his personal accounts that safety was not his primary motivation. By adopting traditional masculine dress and going to war, Robles was living out his true self, not hiding. As a guerrilla fighter, Robles discovered "the sensation of being completely free." Regardless of when he began externally showing his transition, Robles was well established as a man by his midtwenties.

Robles clearly embodied the ideal revolutionary soldier. He was courageous and often daring, "responding to aggression immediately and violently." His comrades "admired his precise emulation of a masculinity understood as a display of strength and violence." In many ways, Robles both confirmed Mexican gendered stereotypes of behavior while simultaneously confounding them by the very nature of his existence.

In response to Zapata's Plan of Ayala, Madero sent the Federal Army to Morelos, Zapata's main base of power, to try to quell Zapata's forces and popularity. But the military adopted a brutal scorched-earth policy, effectively converting more people to Zapata's side as they burned villages. Zapata's forces, Robles probably among them, successfully drove Madero's army out of Morelos.

In February 1913, a coup forced Madero out of the presidency, and Victoriano Huerta took power. Huerta, who had led the Federal Army, was not popular among the agrarian class. A coalition of rebel forces including Zapata, Venustiano Carranza, and Francisco "Pancho" Villa ousted Huerta seventeen months later.

The Convention of Aguascalientes in Fall 1914 worked out power relations in Mexico, but soon after its conclusion the country descended into civil war. Robles was still a member of Zapata's army and had perhaps been promoted to colonel by this point. Zapata reportedly awarded Robles, in addition to the elevated rank, three stars for his service.[6] In 1915, Zapata's men initiated guerrilla warfare against Carranza's supporters, the Carrancistas, who in turn invaded Morelos.

Robles's personal records indicate that he was involved in more than seventy military actions during the revolution.[7] However, it's unclear exactly where he fought. Over the next few years after the revolution, he seemed to switch political sides several times. In 1918 Robles recognized Carranza's government, despite having previously fought him, and became a soldier in the Mexican Army. In 1920, however, he supported the Agua Prieta rebellion, which toppled Carranza. When Adolfo de la Huerta rose to power after helping lead forces at Agua Prieta, Robles fought against him under the leadership of another former Zapatista, Adrián Castrejón.

Fighting together led to a strong friendship between Castrejón and Robles. Castrejón went on to become governor of Robles's home state of Guerrero. This was a boon for Robles, who used his friendship with Castrejón to have his birth certificate altered to reflect his gender identity; the modified certificate lives in his record in the military archives (the civil registry still shows that he was assigned female at birth).

Robles suffered several wounds during his time fighting in the Mexican Revolution. A health certificate issued in 1948 as part of his admittance to the Confederation of Veterans of the Revolution attested to six separate gunshot wounds he sustained during his time fighting.

He might have incurred some of these injuries outside formal conflict—the cultural code of masculinity in Mexico demanded upkeep with "constant shows of force." During his life, Robles would "initiate violent personal conflicts that killed more than one person." At least one such conflict may have been in self-defense.

After the war, Robles temporarily settled in Iguala, in southwestern Mexico. While there, he was "assaulted by a group of men who wanted to reveal the secret of his anatomy." Robles killed two of his aggressors, which earned him a jail sentence. According to Cano, there's a rumor that Robles was forced to serve this time in a women's prison, but it's not clear if this is true. Though Robles's gender identity was usually respected, it's clear from this anecdote that he did not receive universal respect. Indeed, Cano mentions that even Castrejón, who had offered Robles support and affirmation, privately referred to him in the feminine as "the *coronela* Amelia Robles."

This snub reflects a more general intolerance of marginalized sexualities by people supporting Emiliano Zapata. Male homosexuality especially "drew extreme condemnation because it was perceived as being effeminate and a rejection of masculinity, which was identified with revolutionary convictions and displays of patriotism." Gay men were read as rejecting Mexican nationalism in this context—dangerous ground during a revolution. Robles probably avoided the worst of homophobic violence by voicing and acting on his attraction to women, proving himself as masculine enough. Robles's features were androgenous enough that he probably passed for male easily; it's possible that some of his Zapatista comrades had no idea he'd transitioned in adulthood.

Robles was seen as "a macho among machos." In addition to upholding standards of bravery and courage, he eventually adopted many of the negative stereotypes of *machismo* culture: Robles became a heavy drinker, a womanizer, was authoritarian in his relationships, and rarely took responsibility for his role in conflicts.

In the immediate postrevolutionary period, Robles began a relationship with Ángela Torres, with whom he adopted a daughter. Torres may have been the schoolmate whom Robles had had a romantic relationship with before transitioning. By some accounts, the two were married, though it's hard to tell if this ceremony was legal or not because of the uneven modifications to his gender identity in official records. Together they adopted a daughter named Regula, who eventually became estranged from both her adopted parents.[8] Robles later became involved with Guadalupe Barón, whom he remained with at least into the late 1970s.

During and after the war, Robles remained engaged in politics, though he never held office. He was part of the Socialist Party of Guerrero, a delegate of the Central League of Agrarian Communities in Xochipala, a member of the National Confederation of Veterans of the Revolution, and a member of the Ranchers' Association of Zumpango del Río. Importantly, each membership came with an identity card that confirmed Robles's masculinity. The 1917 constitution had not granted women the right to be members of civil organizations on the basis that their thinking was "too elementary."[9] That Robles participated in such groups shows the general acceptance of his masculinity.

In 1974, Robles was finally decorated as a *veterano* of the Mexican Revolution, though the award did not acknowledge the rank of colonel that he had been given in the Zapatista army. Zapata's forces had come to be seen "not as a professional military body" but as "rebel groups of men gathered around their leaders with no systematic procedures for promotion." Because of this, Robles did not receive a military pension from the Mexican government. Nevertheless, this decoration made him the first transgender person to be formally recognized by the Mexican government.[10]

At some point, Robles returned to Xochipala, where he had grown up. His family still owned land there, and he returned to it to work it. Torres continued to visit him on occasion, often bringing food when Robles became too weak to take care of himself.

Robles both confirmed
Mexican gendered stereo-
types of behavior while
simultaneously confounding
them by the very nature
of his existence.

A famous studio portrait of Robles offers information on how he saw himself. In it, Robles's lit cigarette suggests his cosmopolitan attitude, and the pistol he draws attention to with a hand placed on it is a symbol of virility and masculinity. He wears a fine suit and gazes comfortably into the camera. The overall effect is of a person comfortable in his skin. Importantly, neither the pistol nor cigarette is a prop borrowed from the studio. In this photo we see the real Amelio, the way he wanted to be seen.

It's worth noting, however, that Robles didn't have the language for his gender that we have today. He never called himself a transgendered male because that term was only popularized in the 1990s, after his death. Some may be tempted to see him as a very butch lesbian or a particularly androgynous tomboy. His friends and family referred to him as a man, and he used male-gendered adjectives to describe himself. He is recorded by the Mexican Ministry of National Defense as a *veterano* of the revolution, not a *veterana*, indicating that he was seen and accepted as a man by his fellow revolutionaries. His identity, like nearly all personal identities, was constructed carefully, bound and bolstered by the feedback of allies and comrades.

Robles's "transgendering questioned the naturalness attributed to the feminine and the masculine, and subverted the ingrained notion of gender identity as an immediate and unavoidable consequence." It was well known in his local community that he'd been assigned female at birth, but people referred to him as a man regardless because they knew that Robles preferred it. Acquaintances described him as lacking femininity. His nieces and grand-nieces "addressed him as uncle or grandfather." In the 1920s, an article in *El Universal*, the Mexico City newspaper with the highest national circulation at the time, published a story and photo of Robles. Though it outed him, it also became a "proclamation of Robes's virility," and he kept a copy of the story until he died.

However, by the 1980s, his transgender identity was effectively erased. A growing (and necessary) acknowledgment of the women who participated in the Mexican Revolution lumped Robles in with the women, dismissing his masculinization, his status as a *veterano*, and his reputation as the village dandy. In his hometown, he was commemorated for his revolutionary efforts with an elementary school christened with his dead name and title—Coronela Amelia Robles. The Amelia Robles Museum-House opened in 1989, just five years after his death. Despite living seventy of his more than ninety years with the masculine identity he had painstakingly sculpted, his tombstone reads "Here lies the remains of *la coronela Zapatista*." This is erasure at the most fundamental level, done with the collaboration of his family.

There are some rumors that, on his deathbed, Robles requested the re-feminization, perhaps to help remand his soul to heaven. There are a few issues with this, though. Robles isn't known for having been particularly religious during his lifetime; while deathbed conversions aren't out of the realm of possibility, it seems unlikely for someone so strong-willed in their lifetime.

Robles died on December 9, 1984, of old age. He was one of the longest surviving veterans of the Mexican Revolution and is remembered for the fierce revolutionary spirit he carried with him in all aspects of his life.

Joe Carstairs

February 2, 1900 – December 18, 1993

I N THE 1920S, the new sport of speedboat racing in the United States and Europe was dominated by Joe Carstairs, a woman whose audacious feats earned her several titles and the sobriquet "the fastest woman on water." History forgot her after she stopped racing, but Joe used her fame and fortune to push the envelope of gender norms, sexuality, and British-Bahamian relations in the twentieth century.

Born Marion Barbara Carstairs in London on February 1, 1900, her parents were Scottish Army officer Captain Albert Carstairs and Frances Evelyn Bostwick, an American heiress to the Standard Oil fortune. The couple divorced soon after her birth, and she never knew her father. Her relationship with her mother was strained—Evelyn was a hard drinker and struggled with addiction. She was capricious with her affection, alternately bored of Joe or firing nannies Joe was close to, rendering her childhood chaotic.

When Carstairs was eleven, she was sent to New York for boarding school. By all accounts, this happened because Carstairs didn't get along with Evelyn's second husband, who found her too "wild," clearly a euphemism for behavior that seemed too traditionally "masculine."[1] In 1915, Evelyn married her third husband, a French count and sublieutenant named Roger de Perigny. He and Joe adored each other—she once said, "I was like his son almost. He thought I was the end."[2] When she visited them on school holidays, Perigny treated her like a boy: he offered her cigars, introduced her to his mistresses, and took her to a Parisian brothel. Pivotally, Perigny introduced Carstairs to car racing.

A year later, Carstairs decided that she wanted to use her new skills behind the wheel to join the Allied effort on the western front of World War I. She begged her grandmother, Helen Celia Bostwick, to help. Bostwick, a respected New York benefactor, was as determined as she was wealthy and persuaded the American Red Cross to send Carstairs to drive ambulances in France. At just seventeen years old, Carstairs reached Paris before America formally entered the war in April 1917.

It was in Paris that Carstairs first fell for a woman: Dolly Wilde, Oscar Wilde's niece. She was five years older than Carstairs, and the difference was stark. Paris was a bohemian, sexually open city where Dolly flourished, but Carstairs floundered because she was shy and unsure; she later described herself as "too nondescript" for the sophisticated Parisians. But Dolly taught Carstairs how to transform her gauche American habits into charm. Carstairs later cited Dolly as one of the four women who changed her life.

While Carstairs was in Paris, so was her mother. Evelyn was working at the College de France as a lab assistant to a surgeon named Serge Voronoff, who would become her fourth and final husband. (Coincidentally, her work made Evelyn the first woman ever admitted to the college.) In 1918, Evelyn summoned Joe to her rooms and told her, "I know about you....You are a lesbian. I've heard all about it."[3] She put her foot down—Carstairs had to marry a man or be disinherited. Carstairs quickly married a childhood friend, Count Jacques de Pret, to secure the inheritance. She split the ten-thousand-dollar dowry with him as payment, and they annulled the marriage when Evelyn died in 1921.

Once the war ended, Carstairs looked for her next adventure and found it in Ireland, where Sinn Féin, the Irish political organization, was waging a guerrilla war against the British. Carstairs enlisted in Britain's Women's Legion Transport Section, a band of women serving as drivers to officers. She rarely acknowledged the dangers of this work. Instead, when she reminisced, she focused on adventures, like sneaking out of barracks to steal a Sinn Féin flag.

In 1919, she volunteered to return to France and relieve male drivers clearing battlefields and transporting patients after World War I. The job required more than driving skills: due to the bombing, hills had lost up to ten meters in height and roads were full of craters. Tires were punctured, brakes gave out, and drivers were expected to complete repairs independently. Consequently, the women drivers wore boiler suits to work, a more masculine outfit than women were usually permitted to wear. Carstairs found this more comfortable than traditional women's clothing and went on wearing similar clothes after she was relieved.

After returning to England, Carstairs picked up odd jobs. Though she always worked, Carstairs had a secret—she had an annual income from her deceased grandfather, Jabez Bostwick, of $145,000, nearly 2.3 million in 2022 dollars. Access to wealth freed her to remain single and safely embody a masculine lifestyle. The apprehension she'd felt in Paris faded, and she quickly became a mainstay of London's gay culture, dating women more openly than before.

Carstairs pooled some of her money with a few female friends who knew cars from volunteering in the war. They created a chauffeuring business they christened X Garage, named for the fact that they were "an unknown quantity."[4] They hired only female drivers, bought a handful of luxurious Daimlers, and bribed concierges to recommend them to hotel customers. In newspapers, the "garage girls" were photographed in oil-stained boiler suits, grinning as they changed tires.[5]

The business was a success. The women offered expeditions to Imperial War Graves Commission cemeteries plus tours around the UK. X Garage was popular and had notable clients, including James Barrie, author of *Peter Pan*, and the sultan of Perak. But the novelty of a female driver confused passengers who weren't sure if they should treat their drivers as if they were servants or equals.[6]

This confusion of status delighted Carstairs. She was a woman often confused for a man and an heiress in the costume of a servant. When she drove, she served her customers but was in control of them. Drivers could be rented out with the car for weeks at a time, but they also had a level of independence most women could only dream of.

Throughout the 1920s, fashion became increasingly androgynous. Waistlines dropped, erasing the image of a female bust. Men's clothes started to be cut for women's bodies. There was a fashion for the Oxford bags—pants with very wide legs that removed any hint of the female form. Women's hairstyles got shorter too—a bob, then a shingle, and then most daringly to an Eton crop, which was indistinguishable from a man's short haircut.

Carstairs opted in: she kept her hair in the Eton crop style and wore the Oxford bags pants. Reflecting on her look later, Carstairs said she felt that boyishness gave her a sense of lightness.[7] Today, people might be tempted to apply a transgender identity to Carstairs, due to her preferred clothing and use of the name 'Joe.' But despite her "masculine" hobbies and fashion, there's no known evidence that she believed she was a man. Gender affirmation surgery, then called sex-change surgery, was being established in Europe while she lived there. Even if Carstairs was uncomfortable with the risks around this surgery, she would have had the language to express a transgender identity; she never did.

Early 1920s London was an ideal time and place for a woman like Carstairs. Many men who had left to fight had returned injured and incapable of working again; hundreds of thousands didn't return at all. The absence of nearly a million men from the work force meant that there was a need for women to take over roles men had held before the war.[8]

Around this time, Carstairs bought her first yacht. She began racing and was quickly recognized as a talented yachtswoman. Carstairs was such a rare phenomenon as a female speedboat competitor that there wasn't a women's league. There was one league, and Carstairs raced alongside men. She was often the only woman in an entire competition, many of which she won.

In 1925, Carstairs took part in the Duke of York's Trophy, a world-famous motorboat race launched in 1924.[9] She piloted the boat *Gwen*, named after her lover, the variety star Gwen Farrar. She set the fastest single-lap time of the race but ultimately didn't win.

During the race, John Edward de Johnston-Noad, the previous year's winner, piloted the Duke of York (the future King George VI) around the River Thames. Carstairs had created a stir when she showed up; newspapers called her the "new type of river girl," and the duke wanted to be introduced to her.[10] He and Johnston-Noad approached her boat, unaware her engine had just stalled. Joe, nervous that she would be disqualified if it looked like she was accepting help, shouted at them, "Fuck off! Fuck off! Don't you bloody well come near me!"[11]

Despite (or perhaps because of) this, Johnson-Noad took to Carstairs. He described her as

> small, dumpy, twenty-four-year-old tomboy, who wore short, clipped hair and dressed like a man…The actress Gwen Farrar was only one of many lady friends. I shall always remember Carstairs's tough-faced secretary 'Fatty' Baldwin…cheerleading an ever-changing bevy of attractive girl supporters—each of them smartly dressed and given their own motor car.[12]

This is certainly an exaggeration. No one else claimed that Carstairs had a fleet of girlfriends. And the woman Johnston-Noad cruelly called "Fatty" Baldwin was no secretary; she was Carstairs's girlfriend.

There's little historical record of Ruth Baldwin, which is a tragedy because she was the girlfriend with whom Carstairs shared the most intimate relationship. We know she was a few years younger than Carstairs and into wild parties. For Christmas 1925, Baldwin gave Carstairs a foot-tall stuffed leather doll. His limbs were jointed, so he could be turned and posed in expressive ways, and the soft leather of his face was contoured. Carstairs named him Lord Tod Wadley and loved him dearly. She bought him tailored suits on Savile Row and had his name added to the plaque at her home's front door, implying that he could be called upon there. Lord Tod Wadley wasn't just a doll—he was the child that Carstairs and Baldwin wanted but couldn't conceive.

The following year, Joe won the Duke of York's Trophy. She went on to win the Royal Motor Yacht Club International Race, the Daily

This confusion of status delighted Carstairs. She was a woman often confused for a man and an heiress in the costume of a servant. When she drove, she served her customers but was in control of them.

Telegraph Cup, the Bestise Cup, and the Lucina Cup.[13] She became the most celebrated female motorboat racer in Britain.

In 1928, Carstairs traveled to Detroit to race for the Harmsworth Trophy. She posed for the American press—and regretted it. American papers refused to call her Carstairs or acknowledge her tattoos and masculine appearance, instead referring to her as "Betty" and describing her as "the pretty English motor-boat racer."[14] Thereafter, characteristics that had been ignored by the press before began to symbolize character flaws. One journalist wrote, "She smokes incessantly…not with languid feminine grace, but with the sharp decisive gestures a man uses."[15]

These issues with the press were a symptom of how the tide was turning against women like Carstairs. In the aftermath of World War I, masculine women with plucky attitudes were celebrated; eight years later, these same women incited anxiety and fear. London, which Carstairs had established as a haven for herself, became increasingly hostile.

By 1931, Carstairs had given up racing but found herself a bit unmoored. Her relationship with the press remained fractious, and her relationship with Ruth was suffering due to Ruth's drug use. In late 1933, Carstairs saw a newspaper ad offering a Caribbean island for sale. She sailed over and bought Whale Cay in the Bahamas for forty thousand dollars.[16] She left England for good, and Baldwin remained at their home in Chelsea.

Various colonizers had previously tried to settle Whale Cay with varying degrees of success. With trademark dogged determination, Carstairs set to developing it, hiring men from nearby Nassau to help her. They laid roads, built stores, stored fresh water and grains, and developed fields to grow fruit and vegetables. In the first few years, Carstairs rebuilt the lighthouse, put up a power plant, created a radio station, built a schoolhouse, and opened a museum. She established an early version of employer-provided health care: she insisted everyone who lived on Whale Cay contribute to a fund that they drew from if anyone needed hospital treatment.

Initially, Bahamians didn't love Joe, but she earned respect from them by treating employees well; she paid men four dollars a week and women three dollars.[17] This was much more than the British government was paying workers on Crown-colonized islands.[18] Carstairs's comparative generosity was a financial boon. People poured in from neighboring islands to work for her, and many stayed to make Whale Cay their home.

In August 1937, tragedy struck Carstairs. Ruth Baldwin collapsed at a party in London and died at just thirty-two years old. Her death changed Joe. After the funeral, she built a church on Whale Cay to house Baldwin's ashes and became increasingly attached to Lord Tod Wadley. She began to write poetry and privately published two volumes under the pseudonym Hans Jacob Bernstein. On the surface, the volumes are practical jokes, full of spoof forewords and ridiculous dedications. But the poetry itself, though juvenile, touches on homosexuality, feminism, and death—issues Carstairs never discussed aloud.[19]

In the summer of 1938, Carstairs met actress Marlene Dietrich. They shared a short, clandestine affair that wasn't revealed until Dietrich's daughter, Maria Riva, wrote about it. Riva helped her mother sneak out to see Carstairs that summer, concealing her absences from her father and her mother's lover, novelist Erich Maria Remarque. In 1945, Remarque made Dietrich and Carstairs characters in his novel *The Arch of Triumph,* but made Carstairs a man.

In 1940, the disgraced Duke of Windsor was made Governor of the Bahamas to shuffle him off the world stage during World War II. He and his wife visited Whale Cay in January 1941. They were both impressed, and the duke reportedly admitted that Carstairs was doing better than the government was in the Bahamas.[20] Soon after, *Life Magazine* ran a cover story that celebrated Carstairs's achievements on the island.

In June 1942, a German U-boat sank the American ship *Potlatch* near Nassau. Weeks later, Carstairs was called on to rescue the survivors. She went out on her yacht, without lights or radio, sailing alone through waters where U-boats hid. Carstairs found forty-seven sailors trying to survive in a borrowed boat that could barely sail with them all on board.[21] When Carstairs got them all on her boat, several were desperately sick and many had suffered nervous breakdowns. Miraculously, everyone made it to Nassau.

Carstairs's life quieted down after World War II. She lived peacefully on Whale Cay until the 1970s, then moved to Naples, Florida. On December 18, 1993, Carstairs passed away in her sleep. She was cremated, along with Lord Tod Wadley, and their ashes were buried with Ruth Baldwin's ashes in a tomb by the sea.

Witold Pilecki

May 13, 1901 – May 25, 1948

WITOLD PILECKI IS remembered today as the man who was voluntarily captured by Nazis and endured the Auschwitz concentration camp to report on the truth of what happened inside. But his life was full of additional acts of resistance to the worst elements of society in the 1920s through the 1940s. A rebel since his early childhood, Pilecki was uniquely poised to take on the Nazi regime's most violent enterprise.

Witold Pilecki was born on May 13, 1901, into a Polish-speaking noble family. Though living within the Russian Empire, the family held fiercely Polish patriotic views. When he was nine years old, Pilecki moved with his mother and siblings to Wilno (now Vilnius, Lithuania), then the fourteenth-largest city of the Russian Empire, where the children could get a better education. There he encountered his first secret organization—the Polish Scouting and Guiding Association, a scout's organization prohibited by the czar. When World War I encroached a few years later, the family moved farther east to Oryol to get away from the fighting. There, Pilecki founded a chapter of the scouting association in that area.

In 1918, Pilecki joined the secret Polish Military Organization while he was still in school.[1] When the Bolsheviks attacked Poland, he took part in the Russo-Polish War of 1919–1920.[2] After the war and gaining his diploma, Pilecki enrolled briefly in the School of Fine Art at Stefan Batory University in Wilno.[3] Though he had to drop out in 1921 due to a lack of funds, he continued to write poetry, paint, and play guitar for the rest of his life.

In 1931, Pilecki married Maria Ostrowska, a local schoolteacher. Soon after, they had a son, Andrzej, and in 1933 a daughter, Zofia.[4] Despite his new family life, he remained active in the Polish military and its social sphere. Pilecki established the Krakus Military Horsemen Training program, was appointed the commander of the First Lida Military Training Squadron, founded a farmer's association, and established a dairy.[5] Documentation is unclear, but historians have "surmised that he worked for military intelligence or counter-intelligence in the thirties."[6] In 1938, the Polish government awarded him the Silver Cross of Merit for his various activities.

The looming specter of aggression on the Polish borders, however, soon interrupted the idyll he and his family had built. At this point in his life, Pilecki wasn't involved in politics, but he couldn't have missed the building anxiety in Poland as Germany to the west and the Soviet Union to the east began turning their eyes on Polish territory again. When Germany invaded Poland in September 1939, Pilecki fought the Germans as part of a reserve infantry division. There he met Major Jan Włodarkiewicz and became his second in command.[7] When Poland was defeated and partitioned between Germany and Russia, both Pilecki and Włordarkiewicz disobeyed orders to retreat into France. Instead, they went underground.

Polish resistance to the Nazis was fierce. As Auschwitz survivor Jozef Garliński writes, "The whole country, from the first days of the occupation, was covered by an invisible network of secret activity."[8] New decrees from Soviet or German leadership were vandalized with the Polish idiom, "We have you deep in our ass" (basically, we don't give a damn).[9] Clandestine operations were familiar to the Poles, whose country had been occupied by Russia and Germany from 1795 to 1918. Scouting groups reactivated, political and cultural groups sprang up, and printing presses were hidden in cellars dug out by hand; as Garliński writes, "Anybody who could possibly do so joined an underground movement."[10] Warsaw capitulated to the Nazi invasion on September 28, 1939; by October 10 the first issue of a clandestine weekly newsletter called *Poland Lives* was in print.

Pilecki, with Włodarkiewicz and several others, set up an underground military resistance called Tajna Armia Polska (TAP), the Polish Secret Army, with Włodarkiewicz in charge. TAP had been founded on fundamental Christian values. Pilecki initially "feared that an avowedly religious mission would alienate potential allies" but held his tongue and focused on building the resistance.[11] But by spring 1940, Włodarkiewicz was espousing Christian nationalism and anti-Semitic views.[12] In TAP's publication *Znak* (The Sign), Włodarkiewicz's articles seemed "lifted straight from the manifestos of prewar right-wing groups...views that were disturbingly close to those of the ultranationalists who saw that Nazi occupation as a means of getting rid of the Jews for good."[13] Clearly, the Nazi propaganda aiming to stoke racial hatred to distract the Polish people from resistance was working. Włodarkiewicz talked of aligning TAP with groups that were clearly puppets for the Nazi regime.

Pilecki, who had always "disliked politics and the way politicians exploited differences," found Włodarkiewicz's rhetoric alarming.[14] He had long thought that TAP should join forces with the Związek Walki Zbrojnej (ZWZ) "in some capacity," so that spring he contacted ZWZ leader Colonel Stefan Rowecki to discuss this.[15] ZWZ answered directly to the Polish government-in-exile and called for democracy and racial equality. Pilecki left impressed with Rowecki's moral fortitude and proposed that TAP merge with ZWZ. Włodarkiewicz, who had been counting on Pilecki to fall in line with his ideas, was furious but couldn't fight when the rest of TAP sided with Pilecki. The two groups merged to form the Armia Krajowa—the Home Army—in the late summer of 1940.

It was in negotiations between leaders Włodarkiewicz and Rowecki that the idea of sending someone into a concentration camp to infiltrate, gather intelligence, and raise a resistance network was born. It's hard to say why Włodarkiewicz went along with this plan to infiltrate a Nazi camp when he was starting to philosophically align with the Nazis; perhaps he was against Nazi occupation of Poland but otherwise agreed with their anti-Semitic policies.

The popular story goes that Pilecki bravely volunteered to be arrested. However, there's cause to question this narrative. In his third report on his time in Auschwitz, penned in 1945 before his return to Poland, Pilecki mentions disagreeing with Włodarkiewicz as "maybe the reason I had had to leave Warsaw.... [Włodarkiewicz] had recommended me [and] stayed the case" to ensure Pilecki was the spy sent into Auschwitz.[16] Włodarkiewicz might have presented it as an honor, but Pilecki saw it as a punishment for going behind his back to initiate the TAP/ZWZ merger.

Historian Ewa Cuber-Strutyńska takes the argument a step further. She points out that other TAP members, including Lieutenant Colonel Surmacki and Doctor Dering had already been sent to Auschwitz. Their arrests had not been planned as undercover operations, but once inside, Surmacki had access to the outside world through his work in the camp's building office. TAP could have passed along a message to Surmacki to organize a resistance movement within Auschwitz but chose not to. They sent in Pilecki instead. Cuber-Strutyńska points out that "if one considers the importance of the information possessed by Pilecki about the [TAP resistance], it was extremely risky to expose him to possible interrogation by the Gestapo, which could end his mission and result in exposure of TAP."[17] Once Pilecki was inside, Surmacki was Pilecki's first recruit into his resistance effort and Dering was his second. Clearly, the two were not too incompetent for the TAP to rely on them, so why risk a third high-ranking member of the secret resistance if Włodarkiewicz was not trying to silence Pilecki speaking against him?

Though Pilecki was certainly willing to undertake the mission and uniquely capable of carrying it to success, the added dimension of Włodarkiewicz's coercion shouldn't be glossed over. Pilecki's emotional conflict of a father leaving behind his wife and young children in occupied territory for a mission that might kill him should be seen with this mitigating factor. The Home Army promoted Pilecki while he was in Auschwitz, and he mentions that if that news hadn't "seemed trivial in this hell, then I might have felt bitter."[18]

To get into the concentration camp, Pilecki had to stage his own capture by pretending to be in the wrong place at the wrong time. He was arrested in a street round-up on September 19, 1940. He had papers hidden on him that named him as Tomasz Serafiński, another underground resistance fighter thought to already be dead.

It's worth noting that the camp at Auschwitz had just been built and hadn't gained its terrible reputation yet. Most people knew the location only as a small backwater town. Furthermore, what happened inside the camp wasn't well known outside German command. Pilecki knew he'd be arrested, but what would happen to him after his arrest—and where it would happen—would have been a mystery to him.

When he arrived at Auschwitz, Pilecki immediately got to work. Using TAP's structure as his model, he built the underground Union of Military Organizations inside Auschwitz as cells, what he called "fives."[19] Each cell operated independently, with little knowledge of who else was involved. This way, if one was caught by the Schutzstaffel (ss) overseers, it would be impossible for that person to betray the entire organization.

Pilecki had four primary goals in the camp:

- keep up my comrades' spirits by providing and distributing news from outside
- by organizing, whenever possible, additional food and distributing clothes amongst members
- send information out of the camp; and, as the crowning glory
- prepare our own detachments to take over the camp when the time came.[20]

Pilecki made sure to build cells within the camp's hospital, vegetable store, and building office. Each was important because workers in each had access to medicine, extra food, and the outside world. The building office was key for getting information out of the camp because it was the last stop in Auschwitz for prisoners being released. There, they picked up any possessions that had been confiscated upon arrival, which gave the underground a chance to pass one last conversation out of the camp.

Pilecki's work was made possible in part by the shortage of German soldiers working in the concentration camps. Trusted soldiers were needed on the front, so a lot of the camp's internal bureaucracy was handled by German criminal prisoners, sometimes referred to as "trusties."[21] Since they had spent time in prison, they were trusted to know how to run one. They were given permission to use violence against the other prisoners to keep the camp running smoothly. Prisoners sometimes despised trusties even more than the ss—they "had nowhere to go, so for twenty-four hours a day they reigned over their fellow-prisoners."[22]

However, as the camps swelled in size and population, the trusties could not manage the work. As Garliński writes, "Criminals were not clever enough to organize huge camps, with thousands of prisoners and many complicated problems."[23] Eventually, command had to let political prisoners, who had organizing skills, have the highest-ranking jobs inside the camp, like running the hospital and organizing the building office. Pilecki used this to his advantage—the hospital and building office became the two pillars of his clandestine work.

Through released prisoners and escapees, Pilecki passed reports to the Home Army on horrific camp conditions as well as the progress of his network. It's in the nature of secret reports to not be written down, so no reports survive for historians to examine, but we know that he was soon asking the Home Army to liberate Auschwitz. Pilecki was sure that if they set a date and brought weapons, the various underground networks within Auschwitz (there was more than just Pilecki's) would work together to fight from the inside.

But the Home Army remained silent. From the vantage of the modern era, we know the army believed it could not liberate Auschwitz because it had neither the weaponry to fight nor the resources to house and care for thousands of injured prisoners. It needed the government-in-exile to lobby either the English or the American forces for a weapons drop, but nothing was forthcoming. However, Pilecki didn't know this, and, with mounting concern that the Home Army was forgetting Auschwitz, he decided to break out on April 26, 1943. He'd been inside Auschwitz, subject to extreme terror, for eighteen months.

Along the way, Pilecki and the people he escaped with were sheltered by dozens of people. Ironically, one was Tomasz Serafiński, whose name Pilecki had borrowed for his arrest.[24] He stayed with the Serafiński family for more than three months while he healed — in addition to being starved and beaten inside Auschwitz, he'd been shot through the right shoulder during his escape.[25] He also wrote more openly to the Home Army high command, lobbying it to attack Auschwitz. When it became clear that he wasn't going to get a response this way, he went directly to Warsaw to talk to the high command in person.

The Home Army still said no. Pilecki contented himself with caring for the families of Auschwitz inmates and writing letters to people still imprisoned, trying to keep their spirits up.[26] He became more involved with Home Army efforts as well, eventually fighting in the Warsaw Uprising in the summer of 1944. Sixteen thousand members of the Polish resistance were killed in sixty-three days, but Pilecki survived.

When Poland was liberated from Nazi occupation in 1945, relief didn't last long. Soviet occupiers took the place of the Germans, continuing the mass extermination of all Polish nationals, focusing especially on the resistance movement and the Polish intelligentsia.[27] The Soviets reopened existing concentration camps built by the Nazis and built two hundred more camps expressly for extermination.[28]

Pilecki, like most Poles, was deeply opposed to the Communist regime in Poland. He escaped the Soviet terror in Poland by fleeing to Italy. There, in July 1945, he joined the Polish Second Corps. This official Polish military group was connected to the government-in-exile, which was negotiating for peace with the Soviet-backed regime led by Bolesław Bierut.

In December 1945, Pilecki agreed to go undercover once again and return to Poland to liaise with anti-Communist resistance groups on behalf of the Polish government-in-exile. He was expected to use his talents building clandestine networks to re-create a resistance network. He reached out to former TAP members as well as fellow Auschwitz survivors.

In the summer of 1946, a Polish general warned Pilecki that the Soviet authorities were aware of him and watching him closely. Pilecki was ordered to leave, but he disobeyed, and was caught on May 8, 1947. He was tortured by the Soviet secret police for six months for confessions related not just to his current activities but also going back to his work in Auschwitz. Once they learned of his experience with resistance groups, the Soviets held him in solitary confinement so he couldn't agitate others.[29] When a family member visited him in prison, Pilecki told them, "Auschwitz had been child's play" compared to the torture he endured at the hands of the Soviet-trained secret police.[30]

Speaking of his family, it's unclear where Pilecki's wife and children were after Poland fell to Germany in 1939. In all Pilecki's reports, he made passing references to writing to his family, but little else—no mention of Maria, Andrzej, or Sofia.[31] Jack Fairweather's biography *The Volunteer* says Maria and the children made it to her mother's farmhouse in Ostrów Mazowiecka in late 1939. After the Nazis fell, Pilecki visited them in Poland while he was doing his undercover work in Warsaw.[32] What the family endured from 1940 to 1945 is unclear.

After Pilecki's many months of torture at the hands of the Soviets, a sham trial was held on March 3, 1948. The judge accused Pilecki of preparing armed assassination attempts on prominent Communist figures, which he denied. No witnesses were called. Pilecki was sentenced to death on March 15, and his execution was carried out on May 25, 1948, at 9:30 p.m.

Where Pilecki was buried is unknown, though some suspect that he was interred in one of the mass graves of political prisoners in Powązki Military Cemetery. Research to identify the remains in these graves is ongoing.

For decades, Pilecki's story was suppressed. Only after the fall of the Soviet Union were his efforts finally revealed to an astonished public. He was posthumously exonerated and given the Order of the White Eagle, the highest decoration in Poland, in honor of his efforts.[33] Today, Pilecki is a hero in Poland.

Countée Cullen

May 30, 1903 – January 9, 1946

I N THE YEARS after World War I in New York City, there was a surge of artistic work centered on the Black experience in America, called the Harlem Renaissance. Countée Cullen, a Black poet writing in Harlem, was a part of this artistic movement—and, at the time, probably the most famous poet in America.

He was born Countée LeRoy Porter on May 30, 1903.[1] Cullen was raised by his grandmother until she passed away when he was about eleven years old. When he was fourteen or fifteen, he was adopted by Frederick Asbury Cullen, the pastor of Harlem's Salem Methodist Episcopal Church; Countée took his last name. What he was doing or where he was from age eleven to fourteen isn't in the historical record, nor is what happened to his parents to cause him to be raised by his grandmother.

Cullen's adoption was a boon for the young man in many ways. He was given "a new life of books, discussions and parental tenderness" which he'd been denied up until then.[2] According to historian Houston A. Baker Jr., the Cullens probably spoiled their only child a little, but he grew up to be kind and a hard worker, and he remained a grateful son to his adopted parents throughout his life.

He was bright and successful academically: "a model student, participating eagerly in extracurricular activities and bringing home commendable marks."[3] He began writing poetry when he was still a teenager. His first published poem, "To the Swimmer," appeared in *The Modern School* literary magazine during his sophomore year of high school.

After high school, he went on to study English literature at New York University (NYU). While there, he won two respected poetry prizes, a Witter Bynner grant and the *Crisis Magazine* literary contest. Through these contests and ongoing publications, he became so popular that by 1924, "it seemed that no literary magazine could bear to go to press without a Countée Cullen poem."[4]

At just twenty-three years old, Cullen accepted an assistant editorial job with *Opportunity*, the National Urban League's research journal. There, he shifted some of his focus from poetry to issues facing the Black community. Cullen had been raised in a progressive atmosphere and was well educated in the unique issues facing Black Americans in the 1920s; *Opportunity* allowed him to cut his teeth writing about these issues.

The year that he graduated from NYU and began his master's studies at Harvard, his first collection of poems, *Color*, was published. This debut collection secured Cullen's place as a leading figure of the Harlem Renaissance and made him a national celebrity.

The Harlem Renaissance was a 1920s social movement that consciously cultivated Black artists and sought to give Black Americans a unique artistic culture that reflected their unique history and perspective. White American art of this period often left Black Americans out in every form—not only literally keeping Black people out of frame but also excluding Black students from art schools. Professor Gerald Early today characterizes the Harlem Renaissance as a conscious decision within the Black American community to financially support its artists and create a Black American canon of art and literature independent of white America. According to Early, civil rights activist James Weldon Johnson, Cullen's contemporary, "wrote out the creed for the Harlem Renaissance....[It] was about Black people creating great art because, he said, 'No people have ever been discriminated against for long if they have created great art.'"[5]

For Johnson, Cullen personified the creation of great art. His education had been at mostly white schools, and so his frame of reference for poetry was white European poets, especially the Romantic poets. According to Early, Cullen's formal education meant that he was probably "the most well-trained Black poet in history to that time."[6] He could take Black themes and write technically precise poetry that would be well regarded in white critical circles because of his Eurocentric references. He often used Greek mythology to explore race in America; in one of his most famous poems, "Yet Do I Marvel," he referred to Sisyphus and Tantalus.

Cullen's style was considered conservative, even if the content wasn't. He used traditional forms of poetry at a time when other Black poets like Langston Hughes were beginning to reject those styles. Some poets saw using traditional structures of poetry as trying to fit themselves and their art into white structures of quality and power. For Hughes and later generations, it wasn't enough to simply address racial themes within art—to be truly Black artists, they wanted to break away entirely from what white people said was art.

In 1927, Harper Publishing House released *Caroling Dusk*, an anthology of poetry that Cullen edited. It is remembered in part for how he used the introduction to advance his ideas of what it meant to be a Black poet in the United States at the time. These ideas established him as diametrically opposed to Langston Hughes in embracing the Black poet identity and writing about race. Cullen didn't want to be known as a Black poet. He wanted to be known as a poet, period, no qualifier. He saw "Black poet" as a subset. In his foreword to *Caroling Dusk*, Cullen expanded on this, saying,

> I have called this collection an anthology of verse by Negro poets rather than an anthology of Negro verse, since this latter designation would be more confusing than accurate....As heretical as it may sound, there is the probability that Negro poets, dependent as they are on the English language, may have more to gain from the rich background of English and American poetry than from any nebulous atavistic yearnings toward an African inheritance....Here will be no reason for giving such selections the needless distinction of a separate section marked Negro verse.[7]

This thesis runs counter to what the Harlem Renaissance was about, and it was espoused by one of the darlings of the movement. Cullen made this advocation in a book that included many Harlem Renaissance poets who believed its opposite—that poetry by Black authors should operate outside the Eurocentric canon. Poets like Langston Hughes would have been upset by this text, and in fact Cullen drew harsh criticism from his contemporaries for daring not to conform to Harlem Renaissance ideology. Expanding on his "heretical" ideas in this foreword, Cullen wrote, "The attempt to corral the outbursts of the ebony muse into some definite mold to which all poetry by Negroes will conform seems altogether futile and aside from the facts."[8]

Hughes indirectly criticized Cullen and other writers following in Cullen's footsteps, condemning "the desire to pour racial individuality into the mold of American standardization, and to be as little Negro and as much American as possible."[9] While activist Johnson thought Cullen personified the goals of the Harlem Renaissance—in terms of making great art, period—as the movement grew, a lot of Black Americans who were looking for more rejected Cullen's decision not to identify as a Black poet.

It's too simplistic to link their rejection directly to the Black Power movement of the 1960s and 1970s, but both social movements shared an ethos of celebrating the ways Black Americans are special and different from white Americans. Cullen didn't quite fit in. He seems to have perceived his contemporaries' celebration of "primitivism," a callback to African roots, as anachronistic for Black Americans in the twentieth century.

We don't know much about Cullen's life outside of his work. He was incredibly secretive, and little information about his private thoughts survives. On April 9, 1928, Cullen married Yolande Du Bois, the daughter of historian and civil rights activist W. E. B. Du Bois. His father Frederick officiated. It wasn't just any wedding—the union of these two families was seen as an auspicious heralding of the future for Black Americans. There was a sense of dynasties uniting, as well as about how far the Black community had come in America since the end of slavery just sixty-three years before. Countee and Yolande were symbols of a bright future.

The Du Bois family spared no expense to celebrate. Du Bois called the wedding a testament to the "beauty and power of a new breed of

American Negro."[10] Unfortunately, the marriage wasn't everything people had hoped for. W. E. B. Du Bois's letters leave the distinct impression that the wedding was negotiated and planned primarily by himself and Cullen, with Yolande hardly participating.[11] After a "trying" honeymoon, Cullen moved to Paris on a Guggenheim fellowship and Yolande to Baltimore.[12] She joined him in Paris that summer, but by then the cracks in the facade of their marriage were already starting to show.

Du Bois spent a lot of time and ink sending letters to the newlyweds in Paris, counseling them on how to make the marriage work.[13] His letters sound increasingly distraught over their marital troubles. He told Cullen that his daughter was sexually inexperienced and that her "initiation" must have been "unpleasant and disconcerting" for them to have such troubles with sexual incompatibility.[14] In December or January, Yolande returned to the United States and never lived with Cullen again.

Two years later they were "firmly divorced."[15] For many years, there was little information as to why this divorce happened, but after W. E. B. Du Bois's death, the reason was revealed. In one letter dated May 1929, Yolande wrote to her father, saying that Cullen had admitted he was "abnormal sexually."[16] She in turn admitted she had never loved him, but had respected him until that moment; "having lost that," she wanted the marriage dissolved.[17]

Several of Cullen's friends and peers—including Alain Locke, Harold Jackman, and Carl Van Vechten—were openly gay.[18] The Harlem of the Harlem Renaissance was a "queer paradise" where people could explore same-sex attraction with comparatively more ease than other places where acting on same-sex attraction was more likely to be reported.[19] (Homosexuality was still criminalized at this point; decriminalization began in the 1960s.) In fact, there were rumors at the time that Cullen had developed a relationship with Harold Jackman, his best man at his wedding. They traveled together to Paris a few months after the ceremony while his wife remained behind in Baltimore. Perhaps

Cullen hesitated to live publicly as a gay man because he was raised by a minister and still held the Christian faith close to his heart, though that's just conjecture. He was an intensely private person generally, so maybe that's all it was. However, there's also some evidence that Cullen was never very sure of his sexuality and was hesitant to call himself a gay man. Author Major Jackson, who edited a collection of Cullen's poetry, notes that Cullen described himself as "pagan," in his verse, which stands at odds with his Christian upbringing.[20] It could be a reference to his African and non-Christian roots, which many Black writers at the time were exploring, or it could follow a pattern set by LGBTQ writers at the time who looked back to ancient Greece's pre-Christian society as a way to "imagine a less encumbered future."[21] But these "pagan" references are unclear and still not a definitive declaration of sexual preference.

His friend Alain Locke had given him LGBT-affirming material, like the research of Edward Carpenter, as early as 1923. According to historian Genny Beemyn, Cullen wrote back to Locke about Carpenter's work, saying, "It opened up for me soul windows which had been closed; it threw a noble and evident light on what I had begun to believe, because of what the world believes, ignoble and unnatural. I loved myself in it."[22] As Beemyn writes, "For Cullen, Locke became a father figure, someone to whom the nineteen-year-old could turn for advice on 'questions of moral and social conduct,' since he was unable to discuss his sexual feelings with his own, adoptive father."[23]

The letters Locke and Cullen exchanged are full of their romantic woes, including Locke's troubled pursuit of Langston Hughes. Briefly, it seemed as though Cullen might start pursuing only men. But Cullen married Yolande in 1928, and in 1940 he married Ida Mae Roberson. Because he was so private, we don't know much about his logic behind these marriages. Was he attracted to women as well as men? Or were these marriages about keeping up appearances? Historians aren't settled on Cullen's sexuality. There are no definitive direct statements from him beyond what he wrote in letters to Locke in the early 1920s.

With the onset of the Great Depression, life shifted sadly for Cullen. By the mid-1930s, his time as a serious poet was more or less over. After he fulfilled his Guggenheim obligations—namely, publishing *The Black Christ and Other Poems*—he returned to Harlem a seemingly much sadder man. *The Black Christ* was poorly received, in part because of his use of religious imagery. Baker writes that Cullen's "output grew smaller as his worldview grew more dark."[24] He never published another full collection of poetry.

Countée Cullen died suddenly from a combination of high blood pressure and uremic poisoning on January 9, 1946. He had lived his life on his own terms, refusing to adhere to expectations of how Black artists should move through the world in the early twentieth century. In recent decades his reputation as a key figure of the Harlem Renaissance has been restored, and in 2013, he was posthumously inducted into the New York Writers Hall of Fame.

Jonas Salk

October 28, 1914 – June 23, 1995

THE EARLY TWENTIETH century saw two devastating epidemics ravage the world. In the United States, the summer of 1916 saw empty playgrounds and swimming pools as children were kept inside to avoid the poliomyelitis (polio) epidemic. The unexplained disease attacked children, paralyzing and sometimes killing them. Nationwide, it infected twenty-seven thousand people, mostly children under five.[1] That summer, a baby died every two and a half hours. In 1918, a mysterious illness tore through soldiers and civilians alike, killing twenty million people worldwide and contributing to the end of World War I. Years later, it would be identified as influenza. Among the children kept inside for protection was a young Jonas Salk, who would grow up to create vaccines for both.

Jonas Salk was born in New York City to Dora Press and Daniel Salk; each was from a Jewish family that had immigrated to the US to escape the oppressive Russian Empire. The families were surprised by the attraction between Dora and Daniel—they were radically different people. Dora was tenacious, intelligent, and impatient; Daniel was gentle, friendly, and not "particularly bright." Their eldest son Jonas grew up to be an ideal combination of his two parents: bright, diligent, gentle, and good with people. Dora told Jonas that he'd been born with a caul—a signal of an auspicious future full of good luck.

His education in New York included a serious teaching of Jewish law. Though the family wasn't particularly devout, Jonas took the Torah quite seriously, and *ma'asim tovid* (doing good deeds) was a polestar for him. He decided he wanted to practice law, and with a mind toward that he enrolled at Townsend Harris Hall, an all-boys college prep school. Townsend was a magnet school for humanities students, which fit Salk's early ambitions.

Just before he turned sixteen, Salk began his college degree at City College, which was known as "the haven for Jewish minds." His mother tried to push him toward teaching, convinced he wouldn't make a very good lawyer. But he ended up switching to a premedical course; the "orderliness" of science "appealed to him," and in 1934 he enrolled at Bellevue Hospital Medical College, now part of the New York University Grossman School of Medicine.

He knew early on that he didn't want to be a practicing doctor, though he possessed an excellent bedside manner. Instead, Salk intended to go into research and quickly proved himself well suited to that path. After his first year in school, he landed a prestigious fellowship to work in the laboratory of his professor, R. Keith Cannan. There he made his first scientific discovery: a new way to separate bacteria from the culture broth they were grown in. The old process was cumbersome and slow; Salk realized that if he added calcium phosphate, the bacteria stuck to it and sunk to the bottom. His new method allowed scientists to harvest bacteria nearly seven times faster than before. At just twenty-two years old, he published his first scientific paper.

Cannan, realizing what a bright scientific mind he had on his hands, encouraged Salk to follow the PhD path instead of the MD path. That would allow him to focus more on research. But Salk declined because he "perceived how easily one could become absorbed in some chemical puzzle and lose sight of the human element. And that is what drove him."

After his fellowship with Cannan, Salk sought the mentorship of Thomas Francis Jr., who was famous for his work on influenza viruses. He began working in Francis's lab, where he realized that, despite prevailing medical wisdom, a killed virus could be used to give someone immunity. Proving this would become a dominating mission for the rest of his life.

On June 8, 1939, Salk graduated from medical school. The next day, he married Donna Lindsay, whom he had met a year before. Like his parents, the two were considered an odd couple: he was quiet, addicted to his work, and had grown up living frugally, if not poor, in a very Jewish home; she was friendly, outgoing, and from an upper-middle-class Jewish family that had largely shed its Jewish identity to assimilate to the US. Neither of their parents were pleased with the match. But Jonas really loved Donna, and they were both avid humanitarians in their midtwenties; that seemed as good a reason as any to marry. They quickly had three sons and in March 1942 moved to Ann Arbor so Jonas could work under Francis at the University of Michigan's Department of Epidemiology.

On December 7, 1941, World War II barged onto America's doorstep in the bombing of Pearl Harbor. National discourse around going to war was overshadowed by memories of the 1918 flu epidemic, which had killed almost as many servicemen as the actual conflict had. Henry L. Stimson, the US Secretary of War, was "concerned about the repetition of such a military disaster," so he formed the Commission on Influenza with Francis as director. Francis was the ideal person for the job—he had been the first American to successfully isolate an influenza virus and identify different influenza strains.

Salk joined the team in April 1942. Its main task was to create a vaccine that could be used to protect soldiers from influenza while living in cramped quarters. But viruses proved trickier to study than the bacteria he'd worked with in medical school because they require live tissue to grow; for an organism that can be so devastating, viruses can be surprisingly delicate once outside their hosts. Scientists usually used fertilized chicken eggs to grow viruses. As he had with bacteria cultures in Cannan's lab, Salk quickly established a more efficient way to extract live virus from the eggs: by exposing them to red blood cells, which would cause the virus cells to clump together. Once the clump of virus cells was removed from the egg, he could wash off the blood, kill the virus, and store it in a sterile vial. That was the basis of the Commission on Influenza's vaccine.

Testing was initially performed on people permanently housed in Ypsilanti State Hospital and the Eloise Psychiatric Hospital outside Detroit—"the place of last resort of the mentally ill." Without telling the patients, the team inoculated half the residents and gave half a placebo, then exposed them all to influenza using a nasal spray.

Involuntary medical testing on institutionalized people was still considered acceptable at the time; only since the 1950s has informed consent been the scientific standard. The inoculation worked. Only 16 percent of the patients with the vaccine got sick.

Armed with that knowledge, the commission began vaccinating thousands of men in the Army Specialized Training Program at different universities. During an influenza outbreak in 1943, only 2 percent of vaccinated people got sick. The vaccine was a resounding success — and it had been made with a killed virus.

Scientific dogma declared that only live viruses imparted immunity for a significant length of time. Most virologists believed that a killed-virus vaccine could impart immunity only for a few weeks at the most. But Salk believed it could last longer, so he revisited his test subjects at Ypsilanti and Eloise and showed that they retained elevated levels of antibodies a year after their inoculations. In fact, there were no known cases of influenza among the vaccinated people.

Salk made another startling discovery: incidence of influenza was significantly lower on the campuses where people had been vaccinated, even among unvaccinated people. More vaccinated people had meant fewer sick people to spread the virus, so even unvaccinated people were protected; Salk had accidentally discovered herd immunity.

Despite Salk's successes, his work weighed on him. He began spending nights and weekends in the lab, working feverishly. He felt that he had too much to do and not nearly enough time to do it. The pressures of safeguarding the health of the entire US military during a dangerous international conflict left Salk with chest pains and unable to sleep at night.

Moreover, while Salk did much of the work, Francis got all the public credit. Soon, he and Francis began to butt heads. Salk had begun developing relationships with the press and pharmaceutical companies, which was seen as unseemly for a professor and academic. Salk, however, didn't see himself as an academic, and he recognized the power of the press in spreading pro-vaccination messages. After five and a half years in Ann Arbor, Salk and his family moved to Pennsylvania, where he headed up his own lab at the University of Pittsburgh. He took with him increased celebrity, thanks to his part in developing the flu vaccine, and a better understanding of virology.

At the time, the University of Pittsburgh's medical school was "underfunded…crumbling and out of date." But where his colleagues saw a professional dead end, Salk saw "the prospect of independence." Unsatisfied with the university's research facilities, Salk set about renovating offices in the nearby Pittsburgh Municipal Hospital to his liking.

His early days in Pittsburgh were frustrated by controversy around his recommendation to add adjuvants like mineral oil to vaccines. (Adjuvants are any ingredient added to a vaccine in order to "stimulate and enhance the magnitude and durability of the immune response" by making the body react more strongly to the vaccine.[2]) Years ahead of his peers, Salk was convinced that adjuvants could boost efficacy while also reducing volume, meaning more strains of influenza could be added to each vaccine to improve chances people would be protected.

The cliquey world of virology rejected his ideas outright, claiming that adjuvants would cause cancer or deformities without any evidence this was the case. Salk later proved that he was right, but the potential for lawsuits linked to adjuvants had been implanted in the minds of pharmaceutical directors. They wouldn't add the adjuvants to their formulas. (Today, adjuvants are standard in influenza vaccines and many others.[3])

In the mire of this frustration, Salk was approached by Harry Weaver, director of research at the National Foundation for Infantile Paralysis (NFIP). Weaver's pitch was simple: help NFIP determine the different strains of poliovirus so it could make a vaccine and receive generous funding in exchange. Salk, like all academic scientists, needed funding, so he said yes despite having very little experience with polio.

He continued to work at the University of Pittsburgh but received the lion's share of his department's funding from NFIP.

Salk had some foundational knowledge of poliovirus. While living in Ann Arbor, he had befriended Walter Mack, who had taught him how to examine monkeys infected with the virus and how to dissect spinal cords to recover the virus. With this basis and $148,000 in funding, Salk hired a team and joined the effort. Work got underway in November 1949.

NFIP was pioneering a new form of research with this project: four teams of scientists in four different laboratories sharing resources and knowledge to work together. It was unprecedented. And while the organization was less of a focus than the actual research, it was just as much of an experiment. It marked the beginning of directed research, where "a granting agency engaged academic scientists to perform a specific task." The method quickly gained popularity.

Testing required live subjects, and before long Salk's team was straining under the stress of 415 monkeys in its care. The monkeys were often already sick with dysentery or tuberculosis when they arrived at the lab, so they had to be cured of those illnesses before they could be used to identify poliovirus strains. Monkeys, of course, are not usually amenable to being kept in cages, and they often scratched or bit the scientists. Nevertheless, the team began examining thousands of samples from the monkeys for molecular typing, a way to identify specific strains of a virus or bacteria.

To make samples last longer, thereby streamlining his work, Salk began once again using the mineral oil adjuvants that he'd tried with the flu vaccine. The rest of the scientists working with NFIP were initially hesitant to adopt this practice. But as Salk's results began to come in faster than everyone else's and he wasn't wasting as much time replicating virus samples, they followed his method. Salk was probably pleased people finally saw the value of adjuvants, though he didn't always feel good about the NFIP committee overseeing the four teams. He compared receiving feedback from the other scientists to "being kicked in the teeth." They weren't a gentle bunch, which was hard on Salk.

The project continued until 1951, when the four teams were certain they'd categorized every type of poliovirus. There were three strains in total; discovering this "had required twenty thousand monkeys and cost the Foundation $1.3 million." But with the types in place, the researchers could begin preparing vaccines.

Salk was chosen to present the team's findings at the Second International Poliomyelitis Conference in Copenhagen in 1951. It was attended by six hundred delegates from thirty-seven countries, all of whom were working toward a solution to polio. On the way back to the US, Salk befriended Basil O'Connor, who had founded NFIP with President Franklin D. Roosevelt in 1938. O'Connor saw in Salk a smart man who wasn't afraid to go against the status quo: "He moved quickly, found shortcuts, and did not adhere to the unwritten rules of academic research." Salk later recounted that O'Conner "made me feel as if I could see more broadly, more clearly, and more deeply than I could when alone or with others.... I felt I had found a kindred soul." The two remained friends for the rest of their lives.

In 1952, Salk began trying to develop a polio vaccine. He once again faced dogmatic resistance to killed-virus vaccines. Among most scientific circles, there was "an almost religious fervor" that killed vaccines couldn't impart lifelong protection. Salk, aware of how well they had worked with influenza, set about trying anyway.

In just three months, his team developed a killed-virus vaccine from scratch. They tested it on monkeys, and it prevented paralytic poliomyelitis in every single trial.

But the NFIP Committee on Immunization wasn't having it. Despite the many times Salk had already been proven right, it refused to move forward with killed-virus vaccine testing on people.

So Weaver, the director of research at NFIP who initially approached Salk about working on polio, encouraged Salk to pursue testing on his own. Using his University of Pittsburgh contacts, Salk started testing children who had already survived polio once because he wanted to prove the safety of the vaccine itself, not its effectiveness in preventing polio infection. (This time, the test subjects' parents signed consent forms.) When that test worked perfectly, he gave the vaccine to children who hadn't had polio, to test its safety for them. None of them had adverse reactions, proving again that the vaccine itself was safe.

But Salk wasn't going to expose the children to the virus—if the vaccine didn't work, he risked killing them. Instead, he took samples of their blood to get their new antibodies, injected blood into cultures of monkey kidney cells, and then infected *that*. Only when those kidney cells thrived was Salk sure he'd done it: the children's blood—and therefore the children—was immune to polio. He called it "the thrill of my life." Confident in the results, Salk administered the vaccine to himself, his wife, and their three sons.[4]

Trouble came when he announced the test to the NFIP committee. The other scientists were stunned by his audacity and found reasons to pick apart his findings, though once the shock wore off they were amazed by the results. Despite Salk's pleas for secrecy until he completed more tests, word spread. Within weeks, news of the vaccine had been leaked to the public. Salk found himself in the eye of a hurricane of public attention, and he felt it was intolerable. Desperate parents inundated his lab with letters demanding the vaccine be released; the press whipped up the fervor, casting Salk as a savior who would rescue the world's children. Within weeks, he became the face of the fight against polio. Wanting to satisfy public demand, NFIP leadership began pushing for the idea of widespread trials while also making changes to the vaccine Salk had developed. Other scientists involved in the NFIP research were hesitant to move toward trial but were seemingly swept along by leadership's enthusiasm. Everyone recognized the possibility: within a few years, polio might be stopped.

On April 26, 1954, after months of scientific debates, a media circus, and pharmaceutical companies caught cutting dangerous corners

Confident in the results,
Salk administered the
vaccine to himself, his wife,
and their three sons.

like changing the recipe to make it cheaper, the "biggest clinical trial in the history of medicine began." Salk wasn't allowed to oversee this trial. The federal government and NFIP took over, excluding him from designing the trial and evaluating its results. His team had studied around seventy-five hundred subjects in the run-up to the field trial, but now they were sidelined while "a voluntary organization of laymen, not a scientific research team," embarked on a study of almost two million children around the US.

The press, which had once lauded Salk for his success fighting influenza, turned on him as polio vaccine testing began. Preying on the fears of loving parents, it made much of the release of liability forms that had to be signed to enter the trial, never mind the fact that such forms are standard procedure for any medical trial. Headlines referred to the children as guinea pigs and the trials as "the greatest gamble in medical history." This was done entirely to sell papers, and—much like the anti-vaccine rhetoric that cable news anchors peddled to draw in viewers during the COVID-19 pandemic—it wasn't based on real science. It was fearmongering. The press's ploy probably scared off some parents, but many believed in Salk and enrolled their children in the trial. These children, all aged six to nine, became known as the Polio Pioneers.[4]

Salk's former mentor, Thomas Francis Jr., evaluated the results of the trial. Francis, who had always thought Salk was unwise to engage the press, must have felt vindicated when the press turned on his former mentee. When reporters showed up on his doorstep in Michigan, trying to engage him on the trial, Francis sent them packing; when a representative from NFIP tried to get him to loosen up and talk to the press, Francis threw the man out of his office.

Finally, on April 12, 1955, Francis delivered his findings in a 563-page report and scientific presentation at the University of Michigan. Salk, his wife Donna, and their three children flew to Ann Arbor to hear the results with everybody else. Perhaps sensing his anxiety, Francis confided the results to Salk just a few hours before the presentation: the vaccine was safe and effective. The "killed virus preparation was 80–90% effective in preventing paralytic poliomyelitis," an astoundingly good result.[5]

Though Salk thought he was a media darling before the polio vaccine, no scientist had ever experienced the onslaught of press he received when it was announced that the vaccine was a success. He received a deluge of fan mail, and so did Donna. Their house was stalked by well-wishers, and the media reported on Donna's every move as if she were a celebrity. The Salks' house had to be protected by police; the family had to switch to an unlisted phone number.

The public invasion into the Salk household put further pressure onto an already strained marriage. Salk's obsession with work, which he felt as a "mystical calling," meant Donna had been forced to take on full responsibility for the house and the boys for years. This was not what she had signed up for when she married the quiet, studious boy she'd met in 1938.

Meanwhile, the public rollout of the vaccine didn't go smoothly. The end of the field trial meant the end of oversight, and pharmaceutical companies began taking shortcuts with production. Before long, there were recorded polio infections that had demonstrably been precipitated by improperly prepared vaccines. Afraid that pharmaceutical greed had rendered the so-called "Salk vaccine" into a killer rather than a savior, Salk "felt suicidal" for the only time in his life.

The problem was traced to a pharmaceutical company called Cutter, whose scientists had cut corners to save money. Two hundred sixty people contracted polio directly or indirectly from the Cutter vaccine. Since they were exposed to all three strains through the vaccine, their experience was worse than average: three-fourths suffered some kind of paralyzation, and eleven died. The mistake so scared parents that millions of children remained unvaccinated after the story came out. Since his name was so attached to the vaccine, Salk "plummeted from the heights of glory to the brink of scientific disgrace" in the space of a few weeks.

Moreover, though he had received attention from the public for his work, his peers had not showered him with as much affection. Most of his staff quit in the stressful months after the vaccine trials and rollout. Scientists who had disliked his relationship with the press disliked him even more when the press elevated him to near mythical levels while celebrating his achievement. They didn't care that Salk had tried to share credit, nor that he himself disliked the level of celebrity the press had brought him to.

Still, some researchers thought Salk deserved the Nobel Prize for his work; it wasn't to be. Nor was he invited into the National Academy of Sciences, an elite body that included men like Thomas Francis Jr. He was blacklisted, ostensibly for being adored by the public and breaking "the scientists' unofficial code of behavior."

With the fervor dying down, Salk found himself at something of a crossroads: he could lean into fame and coast on his laurels, or he could find a new problem to solve and keep working. Unsurprisingly, he chose the latter.

In 1963, Salk established the Salk Institute for Biological Studies in La Jolla, California as a refuge for scientific fellows making groundbreaking discoveries. It married the two ends of his intellectual interests: the rigid world of scientific inquiry and the gentler world of humanistic philosophy. He coined this union "biophilosophy"—a discipline that "draws upon the scriptures of nature, recognizing that we are the product of the process of evolution. And, in a sense, we have become the process itself."[6] Salk believed that with these two disciplines brought together, people could finally "achieve an understanding of man in all his physical, mental spiritual complexity."[7]

Salk spent the rest of his life researching, including a long search for a vaccine against HIV at a time when most people were demonizing HIV/AIDS as divine punishment for men who had same-sex relationships. In 1968, he and Donna divorced. In 1970, he married French painter Françoise Gilot, a woman equally famous for

174

her beautiful watercolor paintings as for her prior relationship with Pablo Picasso. In 1977, he was awarded the Presidential Medal of Freedom.

In the two years before Salk's vaccine, the average number of polio cases in the US had topped 45,000 per year.[8] By 1962, cases averaged 910.[9] Less than twenty-five years after Salk's successful creation, domestic transmission of polio in the US had been eliminated. Salk never patented the vaccine or earned any money from his discovery; he wanted it to be as widely available as possible.[10] He's remembered in the public imagination as something of a knight in a white coat.

Sturtevant

August 23, 1924 – May 7, 2014

KNOWN PROFESSIONALLY ONLY as Sturtevant, the artist is remembered for accelerating appropriation art and taking pop art to its logical conclusion. By re-creating famous works of art imperfectly, Sturtevant questioned creativity, originality, and artistic genius. She and her work were alternately celebrated and reviled, supported and mocked.

Her childhood isn't well known. In fact, according to the *New York Times*, "Sturtevant took immense pains to obscure the particulars of her own history."[1] It's known that Elaine Horan was born in Lakewood, Ohio. (Fittingly, the name she embodied for her appropriative artistic practice is one she appropriated through marriage.) The year of her birth, however, is up for debate—the Museum of Modern Art lists her birth year as 1924, Artnet as 1926, and Artforum as 1930. Sturtevant did an excellent job obscuring her own background for the sake of her mythology.

She earned a bachelor's degree in psychology from the University of Iowa, likely in the mid-1940s. She moved to New York after graduating and earned a master's degree from the Teachers College of Columbia University. While living in New York, she studied at the Art Students League, an art school with broad appeal to both amateurs and professionals. Sturtevant was described as "fair" and "fey" when she was in her forties.[2] Photos of her show a slender woman, so slender that individual ribs and vertebrae can be counted.

Elaine married Ira Sturtevant, an advertising executive, and kept his last name despite the marriage ending in divorce. Together they had two daughters—Loren and Dea. Dea died young, in her forties. Beyond this loose biographical sketch, it's hard to pin down details of her life with any accuracy. When interviewers queried her about anything but her art, Sturtevant gave a two-word answer: "Dumb question."[3]

Sturtevant created her earliest known paintings in the late 1950s. Patricia Lee, in her book *Sturtevant: Warhol Marilyn*, suggests Sturtevant was still married at this point. Lee called her "a socialite of sorts who had dinner parties in her fashionable Upper East Side townhouse."[4] But she was also a "fledgling artist," and became a member of famous artist Robert Rauschenberg's entourage.[5]

For her early works, Sturtevant sliced open tubes of paint and attached them to canvases. She explored turning them inside out, flattening them into various shapes, even "julienning them into thin strips of metal."[6] The artworks are full of "implicit violence," which curator Peter Eleey, in his book on Sturtevant, compared to Paul Thek's "gory" series exploring meat and flesh.[7] The works explore her interest in "the silent interior of art."[8] But by the early 1960s, Sturtevant was moving on to other themes.

Around this time, she dropped her first name, at least in her public art practice. While she allowed friends to call her Elaine in private, it was out of the question in public. In an interview with Peter Halley, she explained, "I don't like to use 'Elaine,' not because I dislike the name itself, but because it's an interfering reference."[9] Dropping the name "Elaine" had an impact on how her work was interpreted in the fine art scene, which was not welcoming to women in the 1950s and 1960s. Going only by "Sturtevant" allowed for an ungendered interpretation of the artwork, a purer one.

By 1964, pop art, the art movement that examined modern consumerism through a fine art lens, was being critically examined. It was in this spirit of analysis that Sturtevant began creating what she called "repetitions"—remakes of her colleague's work completely from memory. Of her process, Sturtevant said, "The work is done predominantly from memory, using the same techniques, making the same errors and thus coming out in the same place."[10] Her pieces came together as inexact replicas of some of the most famous artworks from the period.

Sturtevant sometimes sought the participation of the artists whose work she remade. Notably, Andy Warhol allowed her to go to his studio and take two of the silkscreens that were part of his own series of *Flowers* and *Marilyns*. (Allowing her to take them, of course, is an important distinction from him giving them to her.[11]) In fact, Warhol stated in an interview in 1963, "I think it would be so great if more people took up silk screens so that no one would know whether my picture was mine or somebody else's."[12] There's no record of this statement being an inspiration for Sturtevant, but the coincidence is eerie.

Using his materials, she made a series called *Warhol Flowers* in 1964 and 1965. Hers are almost indistinguishable from Warhol's. Sometime later, when Warhol was tired of being asked about his methods, he reputedly responded, "I don't know. Ask Elaine."[13] A typically Warholian cryptic response. She went on to remake and repeat several of Warhol's most famous works, including his adored Marilyns and his nigh-unwatchable eight-hour film *Empire* from 1964.

She presented her copies of Warhol's flowers in her first show at the Bianchini Gallery in 1965. Immediately, her work called into question the nature of authorship. By imperfectly repeating Warhol's *Flowers*—which he had appropriated and transformed from a photo of hibiscus blooms taken by Patricia Caulfield—Sturtevant forced viewers to reckon with the concept of originality. Caulfield sued Warhol in 1966; they settled out of court. For a moment, the landmark case looked like it could interrupt the development of Appropriation Art, but the drama faded. Caulfield never sued Sturtevant, despite Sturtevant also essentially using Caulfield's original material without crediting the photographer.

Though her repetitions often looked nearly identical to their sources, especially to someone not told which differences to look for, Sturtevant presented her works in shows in a way that made it impossible to confuse them with the originals. In her debut show at Bianchini, Sturtevant hung several repetitions on a clothing rack, which looked as if it was being pulled along by a ghostly white cast of a man who might be installing them or stealing them.[14] Crammed onto the rack are repetitions of works by Frank Stella, Jasper Johns, and others—reviewers called it "Ready-to-wear Art."[15] Her sculpture at the show is in the style of George Segal, though it doesn't reference a specific work by him.[16] Combined like this, the works cross over into installation art.

Sturtevant later recalled that the critical reaction to her debut show and work "wasn't generally hostile, but that's because it was not taken seriously. People thought I was joshing, or saying that anyone could do it."[17] Some saw her as trying to ride the coattails of more famous and commercially successful artists. In a 1989 interview, Sturtevant said that her choice of artists to replicate was more intuitive than that.[18] She certainly had an eye for copying the most famous pop artists early in their career, before they reached the height of their fame. She might have seen something in them before critics and the public did.

Warhol was accommodating, if not actually supportive, of the conceptual work she was exploring. Rauschenberg, too, was generally genial about her repetitions. He posed nude as the Adam to her Eve to create *Duchamp Relâche* in 1967, which replicated Man Ray's 1924 photo of Marcel Duchamp and Brogna Perlmütter posing as Adam and Eve, Christianity's most famous couple. In 1965, when a Jasper Johns *Flag* was stolen out of Rauschenberg's combine, *Short Circuit*, Rauschenberg commissioned Sturtevant to create a copy, even though Johns could have made another *Flag* himself.

Other artists were less impressed with her practice, however. When Sturtevant took her work a step further and restaged Claes Oldenburg's 1961 groundbreaking installation *The Store* in 1967 as *The Store of Claes Oldenburg*, he demanded that she take it down. She didn't, and the two had a falling out that they never recovered from—and they put collectors in the middle of it. When Eugene Schwartz acquired *Oldenburg Pie Case*, created for Sturtevant's *Store*, Oldenburg told Schwartz he could never have a "real" Oldenburg work again.[19] The rift only grew worse. In *Time* in 1969, Sturtevant admitted, "Oldenburg is ready to kill me" over her refusal to destroy repetitions of his work.[20]

Oldenburg wasn't the only one expressing anger over Sturtevant's art. Some critics went so far as to accuse Sturtevant of plagiarism. But to plagiarize is to steal and pass off an idea or creation as one's own when it emphatically is not. Sturtevant always acknowledged her sources in the titles of her pieces. Keith Haring's black-and-white *Untitled* Mickey Mouse piece from 1981 became the toxic yellow *Haring Tag July 15 1981* when Sturtevant repeated it in 1985. Her repetitions might make viewers uncomfortable because they blur the line between homage and copy, but that's the point. If she, from memory, could so easily recreate pop art, much of which had already been lifted from other sources (Haring, after all, was appropriating the famous Disney character), then where does pure creation begin or end? Is there any such thing?

Some managed a balanced response; *Time* wrote in its February 28, 1969 issue, "If the ideal of pop is to reproduce banality literally, then Sturtevant has carried the ideal to its logical but infuriating conclusion—by reproducing the literal reproduction literally."

The public part of Sturtevant's early career was consumed by fending off accusations that she was copying famous, primarily male artists because she couldn't come up with her own original subject matter. When asked what she *was* doing, if not copying, Sturtevant had the habit of giving cryptic responses that further obscured her intentions. "Repetition has nothing to do with repeating" and "I have no place at all except in relation to the total structure" were two phrases she used frequently.[21] No doubt they confused people further.

Sturtevant's work so "unnerved the public," which in turn frustrated her, that she left the art world from 1974 to 1985.[22] During her break, she filled her time with "playing tennis and carrying on," a wink to Marcel Duchamp's renunciation of art in favor of playing chess.[23]

The eighties saw a resurgence of interest in Sturtevant's early work. The growing fame of younger appropriation artists like Sherrie Levine recast Sturtevant as a precursor, the mother of appropriation art. She insisted that there was a difference between her motivations and theirs, however: "The appropriationists were really about the loss of originality and I was about the power of thought. A very big difference."[24] These are essential differences—appropriation artists like

Levine made exact replicas of the work they appropriated; Sturtevant knowingly made inexact copies, sometimes only appropriating another artist's style but not their content.

Sturtevant made a return to the art world as the 1980s closed, this time recreating the works of younger artists like Félix González-Torres and Keith Haring. In 1990, she moved permanently to Paris. Her work had long been better understood in Europe than in the US, and the move revived her career. In 2004, the Museum für Moderne Kunst in Frankfurt devoted the entire museum to displaying Sturtevant's art, which was an enormous honor.

Then, just as suddenly as she'd returned to the art world, Sturtevant changed artistic directions. She began creating "pulsing multichannel videos that employ found and recycled digital imagery."[25] A lot of these clips were excerpts she recorded from television with her camcorder. They ranged from "comically violent" to malevolent to referential.[26]

She attributed her changing focus to "a shifting sense of selfhood prompted by the triumph of cybernetics."[27] Once intrigued by the silent interior of art, she had become drawn to "the vast barren interior of man, and the dark interiority of language."[28] Sturtevant's late-in-life artistic rebirth spurred even more attention from the art world. Suddenly she was no longer a plagiarist. She received the Golden Lion for Lifetime Achievement at the 2011 Venice Biennale.

Soon after, her work began to take on more overt political connotation. She put together a show in Paris in 2006 that explored hate and prejudice, especially as seen through an American lens. "[American] prejudice is so blatant and so strong," she mentioned in an interview, alluding to living in Paris as the only way she could get enough distance to explore that aspect of the US.[29]

Sturtevant's mission to bring artistic genius and originality under scrutiny seems to have succeeded beyond expectation. Her repetition of Roy Lichtenstein's 1963 *Crying Girl* sold at auction in 2011 for nearly ten times as much as Lichtenstein's original had sold four years earlier. Her version is larger than Lichtenstein's and rendered in oil and graphite as opposed to his lithograph, but, medium aside, the two are remarkably similar. According to Christie's, her work has "calculated, if somewhat cryptic, changes."[30] Lichtenstein's *Crying Girl* has white eyes; Sturtevant's *Crying Girl* has blue; his background is black while Sturtevant's is red. These changes can probably be attributed to the fact that she worked from memory and wouldn't have had an image of Lichtenstein's work to refer to. In 2014, after her death, her *Lichtenstein, Frighten Girl* from 1966 sold for 3.4 million dollars.

Curator Peter Eleey summarized Sturtevant's underappreciated self as "the first postmodern artist—before the fact—and also the last."[31] While many in and out of the art world still don't appreciate her work, there is a growing acknowledgment of her contribution to the arena of appropriation.

Stanislav Petrov

September 7, 1939 – May 19, 2017

THE COLD WAR, so called because no direct military engagement occurred, occasionally ran quite warm. The Soviet Union and the United States kept the peace after World War II through the promise of mutually assured destruction, but that promise often keyed up paranoia on both sides. In various periods, tension grew so high that nuclear war shifted from promise to possibility. On one such night in 1983, Stanislav Petrov was on duty to prevent it.

He was born in 1939 in Vladivostok, Russia. His father was a fighter pilot in World War II and his mother was a nurse. He had a younger brother, Sascha, whom, he worried, his mother favored. Petrov was reluctant to discuss his childhood in interviews, but one can guess that it was unhappy.

At seventeen years old, he was kicked out of his parents' house. In the 2014 docudrama, *The Man Who Saved the World*, Petrov said he believed that his parents pushed him out so they didn't have to take care of him.[1]

Petrov received a civilian education in information technology and didn't enlist in the military until after he graduated. This training led him to make a crucial decision on the night of September 26, 1983.

At that time, he was stationed in the secret city of Serpukhov-15, south of Moscow. He was working on a Soviet satellite early-warning system code Oko (eye), which he had helped design and install.[2] He later said that he knew the system had flaws. It had been rushed into service and was "raw," untested, perhaps prone to error.[3]

A few weeks before the pivotal night, on September 1, Soviet air-to-air missiles had shot down Korean Air Lines flight 007 when it accidentally deviated from its scheduled path and entered Soviet airspace.[4] The Soviets had been tracking a US Air Force Boeing 707 that was spying on Soviet missile testing; they confused the two planes for each other and shot down the Korean plane instead of the American one.[5] Two hundred sixty-nine people died, including US Congressman Larry McDonald. Many thought the attack was deliberate, and the action was widely condemned by the international community.[6] Tensions between the US and the Soviet Union were already scarily high; the incident led to almost total degradation of relations.

Petrov's job with Oko was to verify incoming reports from satellites about potential attacks then pass intelligence up the military chain of command to Yuri Andropov, who would decide whether to retaliate. Communist Party General Secretary Andropov, chief of the KGB until 1982, was known for his paranoia about an American preemptive strike on the Soviet Union. While there was no rule governing the length of time Petrov had to confirm or deny a report of an attack, he and his colleagues knew that the longer it took, the less time they had to retaliate before Moscow was destroyed. If America launched missiles, the Soviets could not defend against them, and they would have less than an hour to launch their own missiles in retaliation. Americans were in the same boat—hence, mutually assured destruction.

This was the atmosphere of constant anxiety Petrov lived under when, just after midnight on September 26, 1983, Oko alerted his team that a US missile had been launched. "An alarm went off. It was piercing, loud enough to raise a dead man from his grave," Petrov remembered.[7] As a lieutenant colonel, he was the highest-ranking officer on duty that night. It was up to him to make the call to confirm the attack or label it a false alarm.

In the 2014 docudrama, which was made with Petrov's input, his character is shown asking for corroborating evidence. He wasn't willing to make the call based on one system alert alone. And then another missile alert went off. Then a third. A fourth missile alert came in seconds later. A fifth.

If it had been someone else, they might have confirmed the attack, changing the course of history.[8] Petrov's civilian education, however, had taught him not to simply agree. Instead, he ordered everyone to sit tight. "My colleagues were all professional soldiers, they were taught to give and obey orders," he recalled.[9]

He decided to wait until Soviet ground radar units at a different command center could confirm the missiles. However, because radar couldn't detect beyond the horizon, it would take agonizingly long minutes for them to confirm what the satellites had reported.[10] The wait would make it impossible for the Soviet Union to retaliate if the missiles were verified.

The minutes ticked by. Two hundred pairs of eyes were on Petrov, waiting.[11] The team pressured him to make a decision. Alarms howled and lights flashed. System checks said every satellite was working perfectly. The computers said the information was highly reliable. He still waited.

The missiles the Soviets feared were headed toward them were nuclear-equipped Minuteman III missiles. The destructive power of one such missile is hard to fathom—it is orders of magnitude greater than the bombs dropped on Hiroshima and Nagasaki. If every bomb exploded in the six years of World War II was combined into one warhead, that would be "only 60 percent" of the power of one Minuteman III.[12] There were one hundred fifty such missiles in western South Dakota, aimed at Moscow, and another thousand were scattered across the northern Great Plains throughout the Cold War.[13] The Soviets mostly knew where the missiles were, but the full magnitude of each missile's destructive power—and how many the US had built— was less clear to them.

Petrov's logic in this moment was based on his understanding of mutual assured destruction. Andropov's paranoia trickled down through the organization, making Petrov believe that any preemptive strike by the US would have been enormous, "an onslaught designed to overwhelm Soviet defenses at a single stroke."[14] But five missiles? "When people start a war, they don't start it with only five missiles," Petrov told the *Washington Post*.[15]

In the docudrama, Petrov recalled knowing that if he confirmed the strike, everyone else would simply agree. He said,

In the general headquarters, all that's left for them to do is press a few buttons. I fully understand that I won't be corrected! No one will dare to correct me. They will agree with me and that's it! It's always easier to agree. I'm the only one responsible for it.[16]

After several tense minutes, the call came in: Soviet ground radar did not register the missiles. The early-alert system had malfunctioned.

The relief that must have spread through the command center can't be overstated. In the docudrama's reenactment, the Petrov character is depicted as crying with relief after thanking the team for trusting him.

In early 1984, a Soviet team traced the false alarm to a satellite that had picked up the sun bouncing off the top of the clouds over North Dakota and misinterpreted the reflection as a missile launch.[17] In *Time* in 2015, Petrov commented on this explanation, "Can you imagine? It was as though a child had been playing with a vanity mirror, throwing around the Sun's reflection, and by chance that blinding light landed right in the center of the system's eye."[18]

However, in the 2014 docudrama, Petrov rejects this explanation, saying, "We desperately tried to find the reason for the glitch. But we never found one. Maybe the universe pulled a prank on us."[19] It's unclear why the discrepancy over whether a reason was or was not discovered exists. Perhaps Petrov wasn't part of investigating the satellite issue, so he forgot about it. Perhaps the reveal of the sun reflecting on the clouds was never a convincing argument to him.

Had Petrov confirmed the attack, the Soviet military would have launched missiles at the US, and the US military would have retaliated with Minuteman III missiles. In those first strikes, more than two hundred million people would have died. Communication systems worldwide would have collapsed from radiation and lack of manpower to repair them. A second strike, which would have been likely, would have thrown so much ash and smoke into the atmosphere that it would block out sunlight and take a long time to dissipate. Complete ecological collapse would have come next, leading to mass starvation after crops died off. Most of the land on Earth would have become desert. Humanity might have died out completely.[20]

When Petrov was called before Soviet command to report on what happened, his colleagues said, "Make room on your uniform for a new medal."[21] Instead, he was lightly reprimanded. He hadn't exactly broken the rules by not passing the information up, but he had waited a long time to declare it a false alarm and had shown distrust in his superiors. Distracted by trying to confirm the system's reports, in those tense moments around midnight, Petrov hadn't kept the military journals up-to-date, as was his duty. When his superiors asked why, Petrov said, "Because I had a phone in one hand and the intercom in the other, and I don't have a third hand."[22] He didn't amend the journals later because it was illegal to do so.[23]

The Soviet military never awarded him for trusting his gut. Instead, he was considered unreliable and reassigned to a less sensitive post.[24] "I was made the scapegoat. That was our system, the old Soviet system, in the old Soviet army," he told the BBC.[25] Awarding him would have meant admitting the system was flawed, embarrassing the scientists and military officials who had rushed it into the field.[26]

Once a promising young officer, twice decorated and well respected by his peers, Petrov took early retirement from the army in 1984.[27] He worked briefly for the research institute that had designed the system but soon retired from there as well.[28] His wife, Raisa, was suffering from cancer at this time, and it became impossible for her to take care of herself.

The uncontrollable nature of that night weighed on Petrov for the rest of his life. He later suffered a nervous breakdown.[29] In the docudrama, Petrov is shown struggling with alcohol abuse all alone. The estrangement from his parents that he'd experienced early in his life became a pattern that continued with his own kids. After Raisa died, Petrov "buried her and was left alone. Deafeningly alone."[30]

189

Petrov didn't become an advocate for nuclear disarmament, exactly. His traumas before, during, and after World War II led him to withdraw from society. No one but his colleagues knew his story from that night, not even Raisa. He lived on a pension and had to grow potatoes to eat.[31] With time, he grew increasingly frustrated with how tensions persisted after the Cold War. When General Yuriy Votintsev, retired commander of the Soviet Air Defense's missile defense units, published his memoir in 1998, he revealed Petrov's role in averting nuclear war. Petrov became a hero.

In the early 2000s, Petrov received several awards thanking him for his cool-headed thinking on September 26, 1983 — but none from Russia. In 2006, he was honored in a meeting at the United Nations, where he gave a speech. In 2013, he received the Dresden Peace Prize.

With his moderate fame, Petrov began to honestly express his frustration about the continued development of nuclear weapons. Whenever journalists came calling, he tried to elucidate the point that the world remains in danger of nuclear devastation. He reminded people of "the inevitability of human error and miscalculation in handling [nuclear weapons], especially at a time when politicians begin to threaten war rather than talk about peace."[32]

In the docudrama, Petrov often reflected on seeing tensions between the US and Russia escalate again. It was clear that he was frustrated that each side still didn't seem to understand that the other was not angry, but afraid. "It's sickening to live in an atmosphere of animosity and old hate," Petrov said.[33]

In his acceptance speech for the UN Dresden Peace Prize speech, Petrov stated,

> Our world was never closer to complete catastrophe than it was in 1983! Even the tiniest spark could have meant the destruction of our civilization! That's why we all have to remember — as long as both sides keep their nuclear arsenals, the danger of nuclear war can't be excluded.[34]

Stanislav Petrov died on May 19, 2017, in Fryazino, a suburb of Moscow. His death was not widely reported at the time but was later confirmed by his son, Dmitri.[35] The docudrama shows Petrov reconnecting with his mother after the death of his younger brother; the two hadn't had contact since his wife's death in 1997.

Many reports on Petrov made him out to be a grumpy man and unpleasant to deal with. He was prone to outbursts of anger and frustration, especially when discussing his estranged family. He could be especially infuriated by talk of the Cold War that focused on the American or Soviet military might. The docudrama shows him snapping at a young North Dakota park ranger who shows more excitement than consideration for how terrifying the launch of a single Minuteman missile would have been. Petrov's generation lived with that knowledge every day, and many were scarred by fear of nuclear warfare.

Unlike many, Petrov never forgot the terror of that night. Children taught duck-and-cover routines in school have come to laugh it off in adulthood, but Petrov's experience was no joke. He had held the power to initiate nuclear holocaust in his hands. He knew he could have been wrong; he later said he made a fifty-fifty guess.[36] It would have been so simple to make the destructive choice, and Petrov never stopped seeing that possibility in every saber-rattling politician. Petrov famously said on numerous occasions that he was not a hero: "I was just at the right place at the right time."[37]

Wangari Maathai

April 1, 1940 – September 25, 2011

RECOVERY FROM COLONIAL rule never happens in a straight line. The process is messy and often fraught with differing viewpoints on what independent rule should look like. The recovery of Kenya was no exception to this. When the Republic of Kenya gained full independence in 1964, a corrupt authoritarian regime came to power, forcing people like Wangari Maathai to stand up to strong rulers at great personal risk.

Maathai was born in Ihithe, a small Kenyan village, on April Fools' Day, 1940, an ill-omened start that she always viewed as "rather amusing, given the struggles she faced."[1] Her mother, Wanjiru "Lydia" Kibicho, was the second of her father's four wives, and their blended family counted eleven total children. Her father, Muta Njugi, worked on a white settler's farm in the White Highlands in southwest Kenya. The family moved from Ihithe to be close to him, and so Maathai lived on the farm from 1943 to 1947, where she learned English and helped with the family garden. Though he hadn't received much formal education, Njugi wanted his sons to be educated, so he sent the family back to the village so they could go to school.

Traditionally, girls in Kenya didn't attend school with boys. But Maathai's brother innocently asked their mother why she couldn't come with them. Breaking with convention, her mother decided on the spot to let her attend with them. So, Maathai attended primary school at the local school with her brothers, where she learned to read and write.

When she was eleven, she was sent to St. Cecilia's Intermediate School, a Catholic boarding school, where she learned to speak English fluently and converted to Catholicism.[2] St. Cecilia's provided a far superior education to what she would have received elsewhere in Kenya; by attending Maathai joined the ranks of a small and privileged class of women "for whom education might result in social mobility."[3] That her family could afford the tuition is a signal of her father's standing as a chauffeur—historian Tabitha Kanogo calls him a member of an emerging "Black labor 'aristocracy,' whose members were better paid compared to ordinary field hands."[4] (These were the jobs available to native Kenyans under English colonial rule.)

In addition to being an enclave of education, the school kept her safe during the uprisings of the mid-1950s. Called the Mau Mau rebellion by the British, the insurgency of the Kenya Land and Freedom Army was meant to drive out colonial rule. In the nearly sixty years of British presence in Kenya, several tribes had become disheartened by repeated betrayals and humiliations; guerrilla warfare seemed like their only option.[5] The rebellion was ultimately unsuccessful, but while the fighting went on Indigenous Kenyans were rounded up into camps specially built to contain them. They lived "surrounded by spiked ditches and under surveillance from watchtowers"; the comparison to Jewish ghettos seems inevitable.[6] Even after the fighting ended and Kenyans were freed from the hastily built camps, some were permanently displaced because the British had seized their land and deforested it. Living at St. Cecilia's meant that Maathai was mostly spared this trauma, though she did visit a camp where her mother lived.

After finishing intermediary school, she was admitted to Loreto Girls' High School, which was run by Irish Catholic nuns. For women lucky enough to receive an education in Kenya, high school was usually the final stop.

There were few universities in sub-Saharan Africa, so most people wishing to pursue higher-level education went to Europe, the United States, or the Soviet Union. These would have been unaffordable for Maathai without receiving a scholarship at Mount St. Scholastica College (now Benedictine College) in Kansas. There, she earned a bachelor's in biological science.

Maathai reflected in a 1995 speech to the UN World Women's Conference, "The privilege of a higher education, especially outside Africa, broadened my original horizon and encouraged me to focus on the environment, women and development."[7] After receiving bachelor's and master's degrees, Maathai attended the University of Nairobi to complete her doctoral work. When she was awarded a PhD in 1971, she was the first woman in Kenya to earn this degree. She became a lecturer in biological sciences at the university, and in 1977 she was promoted to chair of the Veterinary Anatomy Department; she was the first woman to lead a department there.

In 1969, she married aspiring politician Mwangi Mathai. They had two children in 1970 and 1971; a third was born in 1974. But as her career took off in the late 1970s, her marriage fell apart. The same year she became department chair, her husband filed for divorce, complaining that she was "too strong-minded for a woman" and that he was "unable to control her."[8] When he demanded that she drop his last name, she added a second a, fashioning it Maathai, and went on her way.

The divorce trial was humiliating, and she received heavy criticism because of the divorce, but Maathai "decided to hold my head high, put my shoulders back, and suffer with dignity."[9] Newly single, she found herself with more time to focus on her career.

The same year, she founded the Green Belt Movement—a tree-planting environmental organization—through the National Council of Women of Kenya. During a return to the countryside where she'd been raised, Maathai had been shocked by the impact of deforestation on the land: "The rivers would be brown with silt [when it rained]. That is something a lot of us see in Africa, but many of us don't realize that brown colour is tons of top soil that is disappearing into the sea and lakes."[10] The devastation set off a terrible domino effect: the lack of trees led to a lack of sufficient firewood for cooking, which meant families had to turn increasingly to eating processed foods. Such foods don't have sufficient vitamins and proteins, so children were beginning to suffer from malnutrition.

"Why not plant trees?" Maathai would ask women she met through her role on the National Council of Women of Kenya.[11] When it became clear that they didn't know how, Maathai invited expert foresters to come teach them, but these experts claimed that the women needed a university degree to plant trees. Maathai realized that foresters replanting deforested areas around the country were planting only exotic trees, which was reducing native plant diversity. In 1977, she began teaching women to raise native trees, then would reward them with a small financial incentive for each tree that survived.

It was becoming clear to Maathai that the end of colonial rule in 1963 hadn't solved all of Kenya's problems. As botanist Kamoji Wachiira said in *Taking Root*, a documentary about Maathai, "The policy of the Kenyatta and Moi government was no different in terms of forestry and natural resources from the colonial one. It was, in fact, a bit worse."[12]

In 1989, Kenyan president Daniel arap Moi sought to pave over Uhuru Park in Nairobi to build a skyscraper and statue of himself. For residents of Nairobi, Uhuru Park was a refuge from the "squalor and constraints of their residences or the crowded streets of urban Nairobi."[13] To build on it would remove the only green space in the city. With the supporters of the Green Belt Movement, Maathai launched a "fierce and focused campaign to stop the violation of the 'people's park.'"[14] When Moi ignored her pleas, she began reaching out to the international community that would be financing the project through the World Bank.

Her campaign earned the ire of Moi and his government. They began to insult her in public, casting her as a fallen woman who didn't embody traditional feminine values. She was rebuked, told to "respect men and be quiet."[15] But the international community listened! Supporters withdrew from the project, denying Moi the money he needed for the building. Today, Uhuru Park remains a space for relaxation in an enormous bustling city.

Maathai's protest was a turning point in Kenya. For years, "the culture of intimidation and muzzling that characterized the undemocratic regime" had effectively scared people into complying with Moi's corrupt government.[16] But her singular challenge to international powers encouraged people to follow suit. As Maathai explained, "If one little woman of no significance, as far as they were concerned—except that I was so stubborn—can stop that building, surely this government can be changed."[17] She would soon need this courage for a larger fight.

In 1997, the Moi government tore down 85 hectares of the 1041-hectare Karura Forest on the edge of Nairobi.[18] It was protected public land, but Moi allowed his cronies to deforest it for their own financial gain. Maathai was horrified by this. Describing it as "the lung of the congested metropolis," she could clearly see how the loss of this carbon sink would be devastating for Nairobi's air quality.[19]

Maathai and her supporters embarked on a peaceful plan to save the city. They went to plant trees on parts of the forest where development had begun, but they were often blocked by soldiers. The protest grew, drawing hundreds of students and international attention. On at least one occasion, the eco-protestors were violently attacked; Maathai was hit over the head, resulting in a gushing wound that was caught on camera.

While still bleeding profusely, Maathai continued to try to convince the soldiers that protecting government interests was hurting them in the long term. "If we are going to shed blood because of our land, we will, we are used to that. Our forefathers shed blood for our land!"[20] Clearly referencing the Kenya Land and Freedom Army's fight for liberation, she reminded them their land was worth fighting to protect from rapacious governments.

Though results weren't immediate, Maathai's link to the anticolonial revolution woke something in the nation's military. She recruited a new army to her side with the motto, "a gun in the left hand and a tree in the right."[21] She showed Kenyans that the land was being stolen by "an unseen enemy" and made them partners in her reforestation campaign.[22] Protecting Kenya was not just about external enemies but internal as well.

In 2002, Maathai was elected to Parliament under the National Rainbow Coalition with 98 percent of the vote. She was quickly appointed assistant minister of environment, natural resources, and wildlife. Though it seemed like progress, the appointment was a slap in the face. Maathai was a globally recognized authority on environmental issues, but the position of minister for environment was given to a man with no experience working on environmental issues.[23] She wasn't the first woman in Kenya to be elected to the national government, but truly equitable divisions of power lagged.

Less than two years later, in 2004, Maathai was awarded the Nobel Peace Prize for her work in environmental conservation. She was the first African woman to receive the prize and one of only fifty-seven women to be awarded it. During her Nobel Lecture, Maathai said,

> The Norwegian Nobel Committee has placed the critical issue of environment and its linkage to democracy and peace before the world. For their visionary action, I am profoundly grateful. Recognizing that sustainable development, democracy and peace are indivisible is an idea whose time has come. Our work over the past 30 years has always appreciated and engaged these linkages.[24]

Maathai often encouraged people to think more expansively about Africa's problems, both their roots and their potential solutions. Though she never discounted the role that colonialism played in Africa's issues, she encouraged people to think of these problems as more complex than simply ongoing colonial issues. In the 1990s, during a time of intertribal violence in Kenya, the Green Belt Movement began facilitating meetings between tribal elders and seminars to help people understand their role in fixing the problem. She called it the "wrong bus syndrome"—if people got on the wrong bus and ended up in the wrong place, that wasn't the bus's fault; maybe the route needed to be changed, maybe they should have taken a different bus. Either way, it was up to them to fix it, rather than buying into the fallacy that blaming the right people would end the problem.

In 2011, Maathai died of ovarian cancer at the age of seventy-one. The Green Belt Movement continues to plant trees and advocate for environmental healing around the world. To date, it has planted over fifty-one million trees around Kenya.

AFTERWORD

There's a story I love about a woman arguing with philosopher Bertrand Russell. According to legend, Russell had just finished an important lecture on astronomy when a woman in the audience stood up and informed him that Earth was not, in fact, floating in space but nestled safely on the back of a large turtle.

"What is the turtle standing on?" Russell asked.

"Another turtle."

"And that one?"

"Another turtle."

This continued for a while until the woman—who I like to imagine was a little exasperated by this point—told Russell that it was "turtles all the way down."

Writing this book felt a little like that—behind each unruly figure is another one. Both Huang Chao in Tang Era China and Toussaint L'Ouverture in Saint-Domingue were inspired by prior rebellions and inspired future ones. Scientists like Jonas Salk built on the backs of others, moving science forward so future scientists could do the same. It's rebels all the way down.

True or not, the story of Bertrand Russell being challenged with infinite turtles asks an important philosophical question: What is at our foundation? Surely something is at the bottom, holding all of this—Earth, humanity, et cetera—up. Maybe it's god, maybe it's protons and electrons, maybe it's turtles. But it's slippery—where did protons come from? Who made god? What kind of turtle? The answers don't fully satisfy.

Conducting research often leaves me with the same sensation of unfulfilled questions. Where do rebels come from? Are they born or are they made? I could read every word written on a subject, I could dedicate my life to researching a single person, but I would never fully answer the "why" to what made them unruly. Something always remains unknowable, out of reach.

It's easy to say that people get caught up in social tides greater than they are. Historians used to believe that "great men of history" were the driving forces of their times, then the pendulum swung to believe that humans are molded entirely by the time in which they live. I don't believe either of those theories—there's an interplay between the tide and the people that swim in it, a complex reaction we can't always perfectly trace.

And yet, the questions remain. Why was it *these* people who broke the mold? What specifically made al-Sayyida al-Hurra dedicate her life to fighting off Spanish ships on the North African coast? Why her? Why not some other woman, some other sailor? Had she seen someone rebel before her? How did she know that she could do it? Unless someone finds her very detailed journal, we will never know where her inspiration and confidence came from. In some ways, the mystery is the fun.

When I was coming up with my initial list of figures, I had to answer this question: How or why was this person unruly? The literal revolutionaries were obvious, but figures like Countée Cullen were less so. My definition of *unruly* had to evolve and expand and contract until it came to something very simple: anyone who refused to accept the rules laid out for them.

Countée Cullen didn't invent a new form of poetry, but he chose to remain loyal to his values during the Harlem Renaissance rather than sacrifice them to maintain his short-lived fame. There is a lot of courage in refusing to abide by someone else's rules, even if it's done quietly.

Joe Carstairs threw out the rules of gender performance to live exactly the life that she wanted. She didn't move LGBTQ+ rights forward by changing laws, but she lived happily in the face of people who preferred she didn't exist, which was her own form of rebellion.

Suleiman the Magnificent, a ruler in his own right, wouldn't have been considered unruly if he hadn't broken with tradition to marry a woman he loved. Though beloved in his own time, his love affairs were a stain on his image. He didn't let that force him into ending them.

Being unruly, then, is less about action than it is about a state of mind, a refusal to acquiesce, surrender, or drift along the tides of history. Like it was for Jonas Salk, being unruly is following your gut instead of dogma. It's being able to look into the eyes of the greatest thinkers of your age and ask, "But what if…turtles?" And never back down.

ACKNOWLEDGMENTS

This book could never have been finished without the ongoing support of several people and institutions. The reality of writing a book is that it's not one writer alone in a room with a pen and their thoughts; it takes a team of people and a lifetime of effort. I wish I could list every person in my life who affected this work, but that would be an entire other book. If there's anyone I've neglected to mention here, I apologize.

First and foremost, I thank my friends and family; when I had the idea for the *Unruly Figures* podcast, they uniformly supported my newest against-all-odds idea and helped me make it happen. As this book got underway, they all put up with an increasingly chaotic and stressed person in their lives and loved me through it. I'll always be grateful for that.

I want to thank two other writers in particular. Cyndi Oaxaca-Castle, for challenging me to be a more creative writer and better person for the last twenty-odd years—I wouldn't have made it this far without you. Jesse Neil, for encouraging me to keep writing this book when it felt impossible—now it's your turn. I must thank Hagop Mouradian and Grayson Stubbs for their material support and encouragement as I navigated the publishing world for the first time. My grandmother, Nancy Clark, never wavered in her support of my writing even when everyone else in the family, including me, thought it might be time to give up and get a "real" job. My god-mother, Mandana Soleimani, has always let me come to her with my doubts and fears; she consistently sets me back on the right path.

Without my time at Columbia University in the History and Literature Department at Reid Hall, *Unruly Figures* wouldn't have occurred to me. The environment of approaching history and litera-ture in new ways shaped my approach to both; hopefully, that comes across in the pages here. In particular, I want to thank Christine Valero, my indefatigable adviser who helped me reshape how I thought about my own approach to history. Professor Loren Wolfe once looked me in the eye and told me to forget getting a PhD; "You're a good story-teller, can you use that to bring history into the public domain?" Without that moment, I'd have probably already quit a job as a lec-turer at a university somewhere. At the Sorbonne, I have to thank my adviser Jean-Pierre Naugrette, whose love for Sherlock Holmes showed me how to keep loving a subject while also questioning it. Without that balance, history might be impossible to endure.

I have a huge amount of gratitude for Sam Kostka, the wonderful illustrator of this volume. His illustrations put faces to these historical figures, bringing them to life. He did so in the face of many emails from me that had more question marks than helpful artistic direction.

The folks over at PA Press, who published the book you're hold-ing, have been incredible. Holly La Due, my editor, believed in me and this book long before I was totally sure I was ready. Kristen Hewitt kindly shepherded this book (and I) through the intense editing phase.

Sarah von Bargen handed me a sense of direction on a silver platter when she helped me brainstorm ways to "teach" history. She encouraged me to try podcasting when I was feeling frustrated and lost. Without her reminding me that my research had been pretty dang cool, I might not have bought a microphone and started telling stories.

I have to thank the folks at Substack, and Katie O'Connell in particular—*Unruly Figures* was born on their platform, and they were incredibly supportive of the podcast from day zero. The team constantly proves that knowledge and information can thrive outside hegemonic media empires and ivory towers. That freedom is inspiring.

Finally, every other historian trying to make knowledge accessible deserves recognition. Too often our work gets hidden away and never read; thank you to everyone who has sought to make our shared histories more approachable.

BIBLIOGRAPHY

Amanirenas

Asante, Molefi Kete and Ama Mazama. *Encyclopedia of Black Studies*. Thousand Oaks, CA: Sage, 2005.

Ashby, Solange. "Calling Out to Isis: The Enduring Nubian Presence at Philae." PhD diss., University of Chicago, 2016. https://doi.org/10.6082/M1X34VDG.

Dio, Cassius. *Roman History*, vol. 6. Accessed January 18, 2023. https://penelope.uchicago.edu/Thayer/E/Roman/Texts/Cassius_Dio/53*.html.

Francis, David. "The Meroë Head of Augustus: Statue Decapitation as Political Propaganda." British Museum, December 11, 2014. https://web.archive.org/web/20141231192911/https://blog.britishmuseum.org/2014/12/11/the-meroe-head-of-augustus-statue-decapitation-as-political-propaganda/.

Kamrin, Janice, and Adela Oppenheim. "The Land of Nubia." Metropolitan Museum of Art. Accessed January 18, 2023. https://www.metmuseum.org/about-the-met/collection-areas/egyptian-art/temple-of-dendur-50/nubia.

Magak, Adhiambo Edith. "The One-Eyed African Queen Who Defeated the Roman Empire." Narratively, September 23, 2021. https://narratively.com/the-one-eyed-african-queen-who-defeated-the-roman-empire/.

Mark, Joshua J. "The Kingdom of Kush." World History Encyclopedia, February 26, 2018. https://www.worldhistory.org/Kush/.

Mora, Kai. "The Nubian Queen Who Fought Back Caesar's Army." History. Accessed January 18, 2023. https://www.history.com/news/nubian-queen-amanirenas-roman-army.

O'Grady, Selina. *And Man Created God Kings, Cults and Conquests at the Time of Jesus.* London: Atlantic Books, 2012. https://www.perlego.com/book/117500/and-man-created-god-kings-cults-and-conquests-at-the-time-of-jesus-pdf.

O'Keefe Aptowicz, Cristin. "Could You Stomach the Horrors of 'Halftime' in Ancient Rome?" livescience.com, February 4, 2016. https://www.livescience.com/53615-horrors-of-the-colosseum.html.

Porath, Jason. "Amanirenas: The One-Eyed Queen Who Fought Rome Tooth and Nail." Rejected Princesses, 2020. https://www.rejectedprincesses.com/princesses/amanirenas.

Stela. First century BCE. sandstone, 93 × 40 in. (236 × 101 cm.)| British Museum. Accessed January 18, 2023. https://

www.britishmuseum.org/collection/
object/Y_EA1650.

Strabo. *The Geography of Strabo*. Trans. H. C.
Hamilton and W. Falconer. London: G. Bell
& Sons, 1903. http://data.perseus.org/
texts/urn:cts:greekLit:tlg0099.tlg001.
perseus-eng2.

Török, László. *The Kingdom of Kush:
Handbook of the Napatan-Meroitic
Civilization*. Leiden: Brill, 1997. https://
books.google.com/books?id=i54rPFeG
KewC&printsec=frontcover&source=gbs_
ViewAPI#v=onepage&q&f=false

Huang Chao

Cartwright, Mark. "Chang'an." World History
Encyclopedia. Accessed January 28, 2023.
https://www.worldhistory.org/Chang'an/

Cartwright, Mark. "The Civil Service
Examinations of Imperial China." World
History Encyclopedia. February 8, 2019.
https://www.worldhistory.org/article/1335/
the-civil-service-examinations-of-imperi-
al-china/.

Clements, Jonathan. *A Brief History of China:
Dynasty, Revolution and Transformation:
From the Middle Kingdom to the
People's Republic*. Clarendon, VT: Tuttle
Publishing, 2019. https://www.scribd.com/
book/416290639/A-Brief-History-of-China-
Dynasty-Revolution-and-Transformation-
From-the-Middle-Kingdom-to-the-People-
s-Republic.

Fong, Adam. "Ending an Era: The Huang
Chao Rebellion of the Late Tang, 874–884."
5th East-West Center Working Papers,
International Graduate Student Conference
Series, Honolulu, Hawai'i, January 1,
2006. https://www.eastwestcenter.org/
publications/ending-era-huang-chao-rebel-
lion-late-tang-874-884.

Huang, Ray. *China: A Macro History*. 2nd ed.
Oxfordshire, UK: Routledge, 2015.
https://perlego.com/book/1559230/

china-a-macro-history-pdf/?utm_
medium=share&utm_source=perlego&utm_
campaign=share-book.

Levy, Howard S. "Huang Ch'ao Ch'i-i
[The Righteous Uprising of Huang Ch'ao]."
Journal of Asian Studies 16,
no. 4 (August 1957): 612–17. https://doi.
org/10.2307/2941653.

Pulleyblank, Edwin G. "An Lushan: Chinese
General." Britannica, January 1, 2023.
https://www.britannica.com/biography/
An-Lushan.

al-Sayyida al-Hurra

Ali, Adam. "The Pirate Queen of the
Mediterranean: The Story of Al-Sayyida
al-Hurra." Medievalists.net, August 4, 2022.
https://www.medievalists.net/2022/08/
pirate-queen-mediterranean-al-sayyida-
al-hurra/.

Boly, Richard. "'The Allegory of California.'"
Atlas Obscura, January 6, 2020.
http://www.atlasobscura.com/places/
the-allegory-of-california.

Duncombe, Laura Sook. *Pirate Women: The
Princesses, Prostitutes, and Privateers Who
Ruled the Seven Seas*. Chicago: Chicago
Review Press, 2019.

"Garci Ordóñez de Montalvo." Britannica
Kids. Accessed January 29, 2023. https://
kids.britannica.com/students/article/
Garci-Ordóñez-de-Montalvo/330414.

Lebbady, Hasna. "Women in Northern
Morocco: Between the Documentary and
the Imaginary." *Alif: Journal of Comparative
Poetics* 32 (2012): 127–50. https://www.jstor.
org/stable/41850741.

Mernissi, Fatima. *The Forgotten Queens of
Islam*. Minneapolis: University of Minnesota
Press, 2012. http://archive.org/details/
forgottenqueensooooomern.

Szczepanski, Kallie. "Admiral Hayreddin
Barbarossa." ThoughtCo, updated January
21, 2020. https://www.thoughtco.com/
admiral-hayreddin-barbarossa-195756.

"The Fortifications of Gibraltar." Gibraltar National Museum. Accessed January 29, 2023. https://www.gibmuseum.gi/our-history/military-history/fortifications-of-gibraltar.

Williams, Sarah. "The Story Behind the Many Shades of Morocco's Blue City." Culture Trip, September 2, 2021. https://theculturetrip.com/morocco/articles/the-story-behind-the-many-shades-of-moroccos-blue-city/.

Suleiman the Magnificent

Andrews, Walter G., and Mehmet Kalpakli. *The Age of Beloveds: Love and the Beloved in Early-Modern Ottoman and European Culture and Society*. Durham, NC: Duke University Press, 2005. https://www.perlego.com/book/1467351/the-age-of-beloveds-love-and-the-beloved-in-earlymodern-otto-man-and-european-culture-and-society-pdf.

Baer, Marc David. *The Ottomans: Khans, Caesars, and Caliphs*. New York: Basic Books, 2021.

Clot, André. *Suleiman the Magnificent*. Translated by Matthew Reisz. London: Saqi Books, 2012.

Dash, Mike. "The Ottoman Empire's Life-or-Death Race." *Smithsonian Magazine*, March 22, 2012. https://www.smithsonianmag.com/history/the-ottoman-empires-life-or-death-race-164064882/.

Duncombe, Laura Sook. *Pirate Women: The Princesses, Prostitutes, and Privateers Who Ruled the Seven Seas*. Chicago: Chicago Review Press, 2019.

Fleischer, Cornell H. "A Mediterranean Apocalypse: Prophecies of Empire in the Fifteenth and Sixteenth Centuries." *Journal of the Economic and Social History of the Orient* 61, no. 1/2 (2018): 18–90. https://www.jstor.org/stable/26572297.

Sánchez, Juan Pablo. "Barbarossa, the Most Feared Pirate of the Mediterranean." National Geographic, October 8, 2019.

https://www.nationalgeographic.com/history/history-magazine/article/barbarossa-pirate.

Aphra Behn

Behn, Aphra. "To Lysander." Poetry Foundation. https://www.poetryfoundation.org/poems/50270/to-lysander.

The British Library. "Aphra Behn's Oroonoko, 1688." Accessed April 16, 2023. https://www.bl.uk/collection-items/aphra-behns-oroonoko-1688.

Chantler, Ashley. "The Meaning of 'Scotch Fiddle' in Rochester's 'Tunbridge Wells.'" *Restoration: Studies in English Literary Culture, 1660–1700* 26, no. 2 (2002): 81–84. https://www.jstor.org/stable/43293724.

McMahon, Sister Mary Catherine. "The Astrée and Its Influence." *Catholic Historical Review* 12, no. 2 (1926): 225–40. https://www.jstor.org/stable/25012301.

Salzman, Paul. "Introduction." In Aphra Behn. *Oroonoko and Other Writings*. Oxford World's Classics. Oxford, UK: Oxford University Press, 2009.

Todd, Janet. *Aphra Behn: A Secret Life*. London: Fentum Press, 2017.

Toussaint L'Ouverture

Beard, John Relly. *Toussaint L'Ouverture: A Biography and Autobiography*. Boston: J. Redpath, 1863. https://www.google.com/books/edition/Toussaint_L_Ouverture/BPYCAAAAYAAJ?hl=en&gbpv=0.

Collins, Lauren. "The Haitian Revolution and the Hole in French High-School History." *New Yorker*, December 3, 2020. https://www.newyorker.com/culture/culture-desk/the-haitian-revolution-and-the-hole-in-french-high-school-history.

Daut, Marlene L. "The Wrongful Death of Toussaint Louverture." *History Today* 70, no. 6. June 6, 2020. https://www.historytoday.com/archive/feature/wrongful-death-toussaint-louverture.

Fagg, John E. "Toussaint Louverture."
  Britannica. last updated Nov 23, 2022.
  https://www.britannica.com/biography/
  Toussaint-Louverture.

Forsdick, Charles, and Christian Høgsbjerg.
  *Toussaint Louverture: A Black Jacobin in
  the Age of Revolutions*. London: Pluto
  Press, 2017. https://www.scribd.com/
  book/369360093/Toussaint-Louverture-A-
  Black-Jacobin-in-the-Age-of-Revolutions.

Saint-Aubin, Arthur F. "Editing Toussaint
  Louverture's Memoir: Representing Racial
  Difference." *French Review* 85, no. 4
  (2012): 658–69. https://www.jstor.org/
  stable/23214721.

Willis, Kedon. "How Toussaint L'ouverture
  Rose from Slavery to Lead the Haitian
  Revolution." History, August 30,
  2021. https://www.history.com/news/
  toussaint-louverture-haiti-revolution.

Raḥmah ibn Jābir al-Jalāhimah

Allen, Calvin H. "The State of Masqat in
  the Gulf and East Africa, 1785–1829."
  International Journal of Middle East Studies
  14, no. 2 (1982): 117–27.

"Arabian Horses Spread to Europe."
  Trowbridge's, accessed April 16, 2023.
  https://www.trowbridgesltd.com/
  arabian-horses-spread-to-europe/.

Belgrave, Charles. *The Pirate Coast*. 2nd ed.
  Beirut: Librarie du Liban, 1960. https://
  online.flipbuilder.com/kiwg/sixg/.

Buckingham, James Silk. *Travels in
  Assyria, Media, and Persia*. London: H.
  Colburn, 1829. http://archive.org/details/
  travelsinassyrioobuckgoog.

Ellms, Charles. *The Pirates Own Book*. 1837.
  https://web.archive.org/web/20121107
  115227/http://www.gutenberg.org/
  files/12216/12216-h/12216-h.htm.

King, Geoffrey. "Islamic Architecture in
  Eastern Arabia." *Proceedings of the Seminar
  for Arabian Studies* 8 (1978): 15–28.

Qasimi, Muhammad al-. *The Myth of Arab
  Piracy in the Gulf*. Routledge Library
  Editions: The Gulf. Oxfordshire: Routledge,
  2017.

"The Scourge of the Pirate Coast: Raḥmah Bin
  Jaber." Qatar Visitor," July 15, 2011. https://
  web.archive.org/web/20110715134241/
  http://www.qatarvisitor.com/index.
  php?cID=430&pID=1382.

Warden, Francis. *Selections from the Records
  of the Bombay Government*. [521]
  (563/733). Ed. Robert Hughes Thomas.
  Bombay: Bombay Education Society's
  Press, 1856. Qatar Digital Library.
  https://www.qdl.qa/en/archive/81055/
  vdc_100022870193.0x0000a4.

Manuela Sáenz

Higgins, James. *Lima: A Cultural History*.
  Cityscapes. Oxford, UK: Oxford University
  Press, 2005.

McAfee, Robert B. "Letter from Robert B.
  McAfee in Bogotá to U.S. Secretary of
  State, Louis McClane, in Washington,
  D.C.," January 19, 1834. Despatches from
  U.S. Ministers to Colombia, 1820–1906,
  U.S. National Archives, microfilm
  roll 8. https://catalog.archives.gov/
  id/189276212?objectPage=90.

Murray, Pamela S. *For Glory and Bolívar: The
  Remarkable Life of Manuela Sáenz*. Austin:
  University of Texas Press, 2008.

———. "'Loca' or 'Libertadora'?: Manuela
  Sáenz in the Eyes of History and Historians,
  1900–c. 1990." *Journal of Latin American
  Studies* 33, no. 2 (2001): 291–310.

"Nuestra Historia Y Quiénes Somos." Museo
  Manuela Sáenz. Accessed December 15,
  2021. https://museo-manuela-saenz.negocio.
  site.

Pruitt, Sarah. "Did Cleopatra Really Die
  by Snake Bite?" History, April 26,
  2021. https://www.history.com/news/
  cleopatra-suicide-snake-bite.

Henry Dunant

"Henri Dunant." Britannica. Last updated October 26, 2022. https://www.britannica.com/biography/Henri-Dunant.

Chaponnière, Corinne. *Henry Dunant: The Man of the Red Cross*. Trans. Michelle Bailat-Jones. London: Bloomsbury Publishing, 2022. https://ereader.perlego.com/1/book/3046431/10.

Dunant, J. Henry. *A Memory of Solferino*. Trans. American National Red Cross. London: Cassell, 1947. http://archive.org/details/b29978877.

———. *Notice sur la régence de Tunis*. Geneva: Fick, 1858. http://archive.org/details/bub_gb_JakBAAAAQAAJ.

"Henry Dunant." The Nobel Peace Prize 1901. The Noble Prize. Accessed February 10, 2023. https://www.nobelprize.org/prizes/peace/1901/dunant/biographical/.

"Henry Dunant (1828–1910)." International Committee of the Red Cross. April 6, 1998. https://www.icrc.org/en/doc/resources/documents/misc/57jnvq.htm.

"History." Nobel Peace Prize, August 26, 2021. https://www.nobelpeaceprize.org/nobel-peace-prize/history/.

NobelPrize.org. "The Nobel Peace Prize 1901." Accessed February 10, 2023. https://www.nobelprize.org/prizes/peace/1901/dunant/biographical/.

"Photograph of Prince-President Louis-Napoleon Bonaparte." Napoleon.org. Accessed February 10, 2023. https://www.napoleon.org/en/history-of-the-two-empires/paintings/louis-napoleon-bonaparte-as-prince-president/.

"Swiss Flag." Discover Switzerland. Updated March 15, 2022. https://www.eda.admin.ch/aboutswitzerland/en/home/gesellschaft/traditionen/fahne.html.

Vuolo, Mike. "Let's Resolve in the New Year to Stop Using That Expression About Breaking Eggs and Making Omelets." *Slate*, December 30, 2013. https://slate.com/human-interest/2013/12/english-idioms-it-may-be-true-that-you-can-t-make-an-omelet-without-breaking-eggs-but-please-stop-saying-that.html.

Sun Yat-sen

Bergère, Marie-Claire. *Sun Yat-sen*. Trans. Janet Lloyd. Redwood City, CA: Stanford University Press, 2000.

Clements, Jonathan. *A Brief History of China: Dynasty, Revolution and Transformation: From the Middle Kingdom to the People's Republic*. Clarendon, VT: Tuttle Publishing, 2019. https://www.scribd.com/book/416290639/A-Brief-History-of-China-Dynasty-Revolution-and-Transformation-From-the-Middle-Kingdom-to-the-People-s-Republic.

Huang, Ray. *China: A Macro History*. 2nd ed. Oxfordshire, UK: Routledge, 2015. https://perlego.com/book/1559230/china-a-macro-history-pdf/?utm_medium=share&utm_source=perlego&utm_campaign=share-book.

Sun, Yat Sen. *Memoirs of A Chinese Revolutionary*. Philadelphia: David McKay, 1918. https://www.scribd.com/document/466761032/Sun-Yat-Sen-Memoirs-of-a-Chinese-Revolutionary-pdf.

———. "My Reminiscences' in The Strand Magazine, 1912a Vol. XLIII, Jan-Jun." In *Collection of Bound Editions of The Strand Magazine: An Illustrated Monthly*, ed. George Newnes. London: The Strand Magazine, 1891. http://archive.org/details/TheStrandMagazineAnIllustratedMonthly.

"Taiping Rebellion." History. Updated September 13, 2022. https://www.history.com/topics/china/taiping-rebellion.

Teon, Aris. "Sun Yat-sen: Memoirs of a Chinese Revolutionary." Greater China Journal, June 4, 2016. https://china-journal.org/2016/06/04/sun-yat-sen-memoirs-of-a-chinese-revolutionary/.

Tjio, Kayloe. *The Unfinished Revolution: Sun Yat-Sen and the Struggle for Modern China*. Singapore: Marshall Cavendish, 2018.

Yi Chu Wang. "The Revolution of 1911," Sun Yat-sen; Presidents & Heads of State; World Leaders; Politics, Law & Government; Britannica, January 23, 2023, https://www.britannica.com/biography/Sun-Yat-sen/.

Tarenorerer

"Aboriginal Burials." Aboriginal Heritage Tasmania. Tasmanian Government. November 8, 2017. https://www.aboriginalheritage.tas.gov.au/cultural-heritage/aboriginal-burials.

Bain, Andrew. "The Rebirth of Tasmanian Indigenous Culture." Travel, BBC. October 25, 2021. https://www.bbc.com/travel/article/20211024-the-rebirth-of-tasmanian-indigenous-culture.

Carroll, Shane. "Ochre Is of the Earth." Bangarra Dance Theatre Knowledge Ground. Accessed February 11, 2023. https://bangarra-knowledgeground.com.au/productions/ochres/ochre-is-of-the-earth.

Matson-Green, Vicki maikutena. "Tarenorerer (1800–1831)." In *Australian Dictionary of Biography: Supplement 1580–1980*. Ed. Christopher Cunneen. Carlton: Melbourne University Press, 2005. https://adb.anu.edu.au/biography/tarenorerer-13212.

Maunder, Sarah. "'It Makes My Heart Warm': Campaigner Welcomes Support for Frontier War Memorial." NITV, March 30, 2021. https://www.sbs.com.au/nitv/the-point/article/it-makes-my-heart-warm-campaigner-welcomes-support-for-frontier-war-memorial/e7e904v8m.

Ryan, Lyndall. *Tasmanian Aborigines: A History Since 1803*. Sydney: Allen & Unwin, 2012.

Mary Moloney

"Representation of the People Act, 1918." United Kingdom Parliament. February 6, 1918. UK Living Heritage. https://www.parliament.uk/about/living-heritage/transformingsociety/electionsvoting/womenvote/case-study-the-right-to-vote/the-right-to-vote/birmingham-and-the-equal-franchise/1918-representation-of-the-people-act/.

Clark, Josh, and Chuck Bryant. "What Were the IRA Hunger Strikes?" June 16, 2022. Stuff You Should Know. Podcast, MP3 audio, 50 min., https://www.iheart.com/podcast/105-stuff-you-should-know-26940277/episode/what-were-the-ira-hunger-strikes-98402100/.

"Dundee Elections. Mr. Churchill and the Suffragettes: Amusing Scenes: Silenced by a Clanging Bell." *Irish Times*, May 5, 1908. British Newspapers Archive. https://www.britishnewspaperarchive.co.uk/viewer/bl/0001683/19080505/138/0005.

"Glasthule Baptisms: May 27th 1865 to December 24th 1902." Catholic Parish Registers at the NLI, n.d. National Library of Ireland. Accessed May 15, 2022. http://registers.nli.ie/parishes/0522.

"House of Commons General View, Showing the Ladies' Gallery above the Speaker's Chair" (United Kingdom Parliament), Parliamentary Archives, FAR/1/7, UK Living Heritage, accessed April 13, 2023, https://www.parliament.uk/about/living-heritage/transformingsociety/electionsvoting/womenvote/parliamentary-collections/ladies-gallery-grille/ladies-gallery/.

"In Memoriam: Horatia Dorothy Malony Lancaster," *The Vote*. December 9, 1921. British Newspapers Archive. https://www.britishnewspaperarchive.co.uk/viewer/bl/0002186/19211209/016/0006.

National Federation of Women Workers. "Gaps in the Grille." *The Woman Worker*, November 4, 1908. LSE Digital Library.

Strachey, Ray. *The Cause: A Short History of the Women's Movement in Great Britain*. Port Washington, NY: Kennikat Press, 1969. http://archive.org/details/causeshorthistor0083stra.

"Suffragettes Bomb Westminster Abbey." *Raidió Teilifís Éireann*. Century Ireland. June 12, 1914. https://www.rte.ie/centuryireland/index.php/articles/suffragettes-bomb-westminster-abbey.

Suffragettes Forever! The Story of Women and Power. episode 2, "Episode #1.2" directed by Rupert Edwards, written by Jacqui Hayden aired March 4, 2015, on the BBC.

Wallace, Eleanor. "Suffragette Outrages: The Women's Social and Political Union WSPU." Historic UK February 10, 2022. https://www.historic-uk.com/HistoryU.K./HistoryofBritain/Suffragette-Outrages-WSPU/.

"Who Were the Suffragettes?" Museum of London. Accessed May 15, 2022. https://www.museumoflondon.org.uk/museum-london/explore/who-were-suffragettes.

Amelio Robles Avila

Cano, Gabriela. "Unconcealable Realities of Desire." In *Sex in Revolution: Gender, Politics, and Power in Modern Mexico*. Ed. Jocelyn Olcott, Mary Kay Vaughan, and Gabriela Cano. Durham, NC: Duke University Press, 2007, 35–56.

Martinez Alarcón, Laura. "La Coronela es un hombre y, sin embargo, nació mujer." Actitudfem. March 7, 2016. https://www.actitudfem.com/entorno/genero/lgbt/la-coronela-es-un-hombre-y-sin-embargo-nacio-mujer.

"Mexican Revolution." Britannica. Last updated November 09, 2022. https://www.britannica.com/event/Mexican-Revolution.

"Mexican Revolution." History. Updated June 10, 2009. https://www.history.com/topics/latin-america/mexican-revolution.

Monsiváis, Carlos. "Foreword." In *Sex in Revolution: Gender, Politics, and Power in Modern Mexico*, edited by Jocelyn Olcott, Mary Kay Vaughan, and Gabriela Cano. Durham, NC: Duke University Press, 2007, 35–56.

Zapata, Emiliano, and Otilio Montaño. "Plan of Ayala," November 25, 1911. Library of Congress. https://www.loc.gov/item/2021667593/.

Joe Carstairs

Clark, D. "Population of the United Kingdom from 1871 to 2021." Statista. Accessed February 1, 2023. https://www.statista.com/statistics/281296/uk-population/.

"The Duke of York's Trophy Motor-Boat Races." *Motor Sport Magazine*, September 1927. https://www.motorsportmagazine.com/archive/article/september-1927/12/the-duke-of-yorks-trophy-motor-boat-races/.

Summerscale, Kate. *The Queen of Whale Cay: The Eccentric Story of "Joe" Carstairs, Fastest Woman on Water*. New York: Viking, 1998. http://archive.org/details/queenofwhalecay0000summ_h8z4.

West Indies: Volume 331: Debated on Wednesday 9 February 1938. Hansard, UK Parliament. https://hansard.parliament.uk//Commons/1938-02-09/debates/3e35d447-101a-4eab-91b8-3081ef6a179e/WestIndies.

Wiberg, Eric T. "S. S. *Potlatch* and Capt. John Joseph Lapoint," September 16, 2015. https://www.academia.edu/25038931/BHS_FINAL_Article_SS_Potlatch_by_ET_Wiberg.

Witold Pilecki

Cuber-Strutyńska, Ewa. "Witold Pilecki. Confronting the Legend of the 'Volunteer to Auschwitz.'" *Journal of the Polish Center for Holocaust Research*, no. Holocaust Studies and Materials (December 6, 2017): 281–301. https://doi.org/10.32927/zzsim.720.

Fairweather, Jack. *The Volunteer: One Man, an Underground Army, and the Secret Mission to Destroy Auschwitz*. Kindle. New York, NY: Custom House, 2019.

Garliński, Jarek. "Historical Horizon." *The Auschwitz Volunteer: Beyond Bravery*, Kindle. Aquila Polonica, 2014.

Garliński, Józef. *Fighting Auschwitz: The Resistance Movement in the Concentration Camp*. 1st Edition. Los Angeles, CA: Aquila Polonica, 1975.

Instytut Pamięci Narodowej Komisja Ścigania Zbrodni przeciwko Narodowi Polskiemu. "Captain Witold Pilecki." Biogramy Postaci Historycznych, n.d. https://biogramy.ipn.gov.pl/bio/wszystkie-biogramy/rotmistrz-witold-pileck/english-version/112337,Captain-Witold-Pilecki.html.

Pilecki, Witold. *The Auschwitz Volunteer: Beyond Bravery*. Translated by Jarek Garliński. Kindle. Aquila Polonica, 2014.

— — —. *WITOLD'S REPORT*, 1942. http://archive.org/details/WITOLDREPORT.

Wołek, Karol. "A Post-War War. The Years of 1944–1963 in Poland." *The Warsaw Institute Review*, October 1, 2018. https://warsawinstitute.org/post-war-war-years-1944-1963-poland/.

Countée Cullen

Baker, Houston A. *Afro-American Poetics: Revisions of Harlem and the Black Aesthetic*. Madison: University of Wisconsin Press, 1988.

Beemyn, Genny. *A Queer Capital: A History of Gay Life in Washington D.C.* Oxfordshire: Routledge, 2014. https://www.perlego.com/book/1545531/a-queer-capital-a-history-of-gay-life-in-washington-dc-pdf.

"Countee Cullen." National Museum of African American History and Culture. Accessed March 28, 2022. https://nmaahc.si.edu/countee-cullen.

Cullen, Countee. *Caroling Dusk: An Anthology of Verse by Negro Poets*. New York: Harper & Brothers, 1927. https://archive.org/details/carolingduskoocoun/page/n11/mode/2up

— — —. *Countee Cullen: Collected Poems*. Ed. Major Jackson. American Poets Project 32. New York: Library of America, 2013.

Diaz, Joanne, and Abram Van Engen. "Countee Cullen, Yet Do I Marvel." Episode 28. September 29, 2021. In *Poetry for All*. Podcast, MP3 audio, 24:48. https://poetry-forall.fireside.fm/28.

Du Bois, Yolande, to W. E. B. Du Bois. May 23, 1929. W. E. B. Du Bois Papers (MS 312). Special Collections and University Archives, University of Massachusetts Amherst Libraries. http://credo.library.umass.edu/view/full/mums312-b048-i062.

English, Daylanne K. *Unnatural Selections: Eugenics in American Modernism and the Harlem Renaissance*. New edition. Chapel Hill: University of North Carolina Press, 2004.

Lewis, David L. *When Harlem Was in Vogue*. 2nd edition. New York: Penguin Books, 1997. https://archive.org/details/whenharlemwasinvoooolewi_g4t5.

Molesworth, Charles. "Countee Cullen's Reputation." *Transition* 107 (2012): 67–77. https://doi.org/10.2979/transition.107.67.

"Overview." W. E. B. Du Bois Papers, 1803–1999 (bulk 1877–1963). Robert S. Cox Special Collections and University Archives Research Center. University of Massachusetts Amherst. Accessed February 13, 2023. https://credo.library.umass.edu/view/collection/mums312.

Stokes, Mason. "Strange Fruits." *Transition* 92 (2002): 56–79. https://www.jstor.org/stable/3172461.

Wintz, Cary D., and Paul Finkelman. *Encyclopedia of the Harlem Renaissance: A–J.* New York: Taylor & Francis, 2004.

Jonas Salk

"About Jonas Salk." Salk Institute for Biological Studies. Accessed June 12, 2022. https://www.salk.edu/about/history-of-salk/jonas-salk/.

"Adjuvants and Vaccines." Questions and Concerns, Vaccine Safety, Centers for Disease Control and Prevention. Updated September 27, 2022. https://www.cdc.gov/vaccinesafety/concerns/adjuvants.html.

Jacobs, Charlotte DeCroes. *Jonas Salk: A Life.* New York: Oxford University Press, 2015.

Meldrum, Marcia. "'A Calculated Risk': The Salk Polio Vaccine Field Trials of 1954." *British Medical Journal* 317, no. 7167 (October 31, 1998): 1233–36.

The Open Mind. Episode "Man Evolving." Aired May 11, 1985, on PBS. https://www.njpbs.org/programs/the-open-mind/the-open-mind-man-evolving/.

Pulendran, Bali, Prabhu S. Arunachalam, and Derek T. O'Hagan. "Emerging Concepts in the Science of Vaccine Adjuvants." *Nature Reviews Drug Discovery* 20, no. 6 (June 2021): 454–75. https://doi.org/10.1038/s41573-021-00163-y.

Taubman, Howard. "Father of Biophilosophy." *New York Times*, November 11, 1966.

Stanislav Petrov

Aksenov, Pavel. "Stanislav Petrov: The Man Who May Have Saved the World." BBC News, September 26, 2013. https://web.archive.org/web/20140308000459/https://www.bbc.com/news/world-europe-24280831.

Chan, Sewell. "Stanislav Petrov, Soviet Officer Who Helped Avert Nuclear War, Is Dead at 77." *New York Times*, September 18, 2017. https://web.archive.org/web/20170919023131/https://www.nytimes.com/2017/09/18/world/europe/stanislav-petrov-nuclear-war-dead.html.

Hoffman, David. "I Had a Funny Feeling in My Gut." *Washington Post*, February 10, 1999. https://web.archive.org/web/20181218193954/https://www.washingtonpost.com/wp-srv/inatl/longterm/coldwar/soviet10.htm.

"Korean Air Lines Flight 007." Britannica. Last updated February 3, 2023. https://www.britannica.com/event/Korean-Air-Lines-flight-007.

Lebedev, Anastasiya. "The Man Who Saved the World Finally Recognized." Association of World Citizens. May 21, 2004. https://web.archive.org/web/20110721000030/http://www.worldcitizens.org/petrov2.html.

Little, Allan. "How I Stopped Nuclear War." BBC News, October 21, 1998. https://web.archive.org/web/20061108234104/http://news.bbc.co.uk/2/hi/europe/198173.stm.

The Man Who Saved the World. Directed by Peter Anthony. Docudrama. 2015. https://www.amazon.com/Man-Who-Saved-World/dp/B07DVVKFTW.

Pedersen, Glen. "Stanislav Petrov: World Hero." *Fellowship* 71 no. 7–8 (July 2005): 9.

Shuster, Simon. "Stanislav Petrov, the Russian Officer Who Averted a Nuclear War, Feared History Repeating Itself." *Time*, September 19, 2017. https://time.com/4947879/stanislav-petrov-russia-nuclear-war-obituary/.

Sturtevant

Eleey, Peter, and Elaine Sturtevant. *Sturtevant: Double Trouble.* New York: Museum of Modern Art, 2014.

Fox, Margalit. "Elaine Sturtevant, Who Borrowed Others' Work Artfully, Is Dead at 89." *New York Times*, May 16, 2014. https://www.nytimes.com/2014/05/17/arts/design/elaine-sturtevant-appropriation-artist-is-dead-at-89.html.

Heartney, Eleanor. "Re-Creating Sturtevant." *Art in America*, November 1, 2014. https://www.artnews.com/art-in-america/features/re-creating-sturtevant-63492/.

K., Dea. "Elaine Sturtevant." Widewalls, August 30, 2016. https://www.widewalls.ch/artists/elaine-sturtevant.

Lee, Patricia. *Sturtevant: Warhol Marilyn*. One Work 14. London: Afterall Books, 2016.

Rosenberg, Karen. "A Controversy Over 'Empire.'" *New York*, November 12, 2004. https://nymag.com/nymetro/arts/art/10422/.

Sturtevant. *Oral History Interview with Elaine Sturtevant, 2007 July 25–26*, 2007. Archives of American Art, Smithsonian Institution. https://www.aaa.si.edu/collections/interviews/oral-history-interview-elaine-sturtevant-13622.

"Sturtevant (1926–2014) *Lichtenstein, Frighten Girl*." Post-War & Contemporary Art Evening Sale, Live Auction 2891, Christie's, November 11, 2014. https://www.christies.com/en/lot/lot-5846086.

"Sturtevant with Peter Halley." *Index*, 2005. http://www.indexmagazine.com/interviews/sturtevant.shtml.

Sturtevant's Repetitions. Museum of Contemporary Art. 2015. YouTube video, 3:30. https://www.youtube.com/watch?v=PMhjxwR_-KY.

"Trends: Statements in Paint." *Time*, February 28, 1969. https://content.time.com/time/subscriber/article/0,33009,900703-3,00.html.

Wangari Maathai

"Ghettos." Holocaust Encyclopedia, United States Holocaust Memorial Museum. Accessed February 15, 2023. https://encyclopedia.ushmm.org/content/en/article/ghettos.

"John F. Kennedy and the Student Airlift | JFK Library." JFK in History, About JFK, Learn, John F. Kennedy: Presidential Library and Museum. Accessed April 12, 2023. https://www.jfklibrary.org/learn/about-jfk/jfk-in-history/john-f-kennedy-and-the-student-airlift.

Kanogo, Tabitha. *Wangari Maathai*. Ohio Short Histories of Africa. Athens: Ohio University Press, 2020. https://www.scribd.com/book/453420977/Wangari-Maathai.

Maathai, Wangari. "Bottlenecks to Development in Africa." 4th UN World Women's Conference, Beijing, China, August 30, 1995. https://www.greenbeltmovement.org/wangari-maathai/key-speeches-and-articles/bottleknecks-to-development-in-africa.

———. "Nobel Lecture." Nobel Peace Prize 2004., Oslo, Norway, December 10, 2004. https://www.nobelprize.org/prizes/peace/2004/maathai/lecture/.

———. *Unbowed: A Memoir*. New York: Alfred A. Knopf, 2006. https://archive.org/details/unbowedmemoiroooomaat/.

Murray, Jenni. *A History of the World in 21 Women: A Personal Collection*. London: Oneworld Publications, 2018, 202–12. https://www.scribd.com/book/433020639/A-History-of-the-World-in-21-Women-A-Personal-Selection.

Taking Root: The Vision of Wangari Maathai. BrattleboroTV2, 2008, YouTube video, 1:20:00. https://www.youtube.com/watch?v=G3My-B4NtOI.

"Tree Planting and Water Harvesting." Green Belt Movement." Accessed February 4, 2023. http://www.greenbeltmovement.org/what-we-do/tree-planting-for-watersheds.

NOTES

Kandake Amanirenas

1 Janice Kamrin and Adela Oppenheim, "The Land of Nubia," Metropolitan Museum of Art, accessed January 18, 2023, https://www.metmuseum.org/about-the-met/collection-areas/egyptian-art/temple-of-dendur-50/nubia.
2 Joshua J Mark, "The Kingdom of Kush," World History Encyclopedia, February 26, 2018, https://www.worldhistory.org/Kush/.
3 Selina O'Grady, And Man Created God: Kings, Cults and Conquests at the Time of Jesus (London: Atlantic Books, 2012), "The African Goddess-Queen," Perlego. https://www.perlego.com/book/117500/and-man-created-god-kings-cults-and-conquests-at-the-time-of-jesus-pdf.
4 O'Grady, And Man Created God, "The African Goddess-Queen," Kindle.
5 László Török, The Kingdom of Kush: Handbook of the Napatan-Meroitic Civilization (Leiden: Brill, 1997), 455, https://books.google.com/books?id=i54rPFeGKewC&printsec=frontcover&source=gbs_ViewAPI#v=onepage&q&f=false.
6 Strabo, The Geography of Strabo, trans. H. C. Hamilton and W. Falconer, vol. 3 (London: G. Bell & Sons, 1903), book 17, chapter 1, section 54. Google Play Books. https://play.google.com/store/books/details?id=IfMrAAAAYAAJ&rdid=book-IfMrAAAAYAAJ&rdot=1&pli=1.
7 Cassius Dio, Roman History, vol. 6, book 53, section 23, accessed January 18, 2023, https://penelope.uchicago.edu/Thayer/E/Roman/Texts/Cassius_Dio/53*.html.
8 Dio, Roman History, vol. 6, book 53, section 23.
9 Strabo, Geography of Strabo, 17.1.54.
10 Adhiambo Edith Magak, "The One-Eyed African Queen Who Defeated the Roman Empire," Narratively, September 23, 2021, https://narratively.com/the-one-eyed-african-queen-who-defeated-the-roman-empire/.
11 Dio, Roman History, vol. 6, book 54, section 5.
12 Strabo, Geography of Strabo, 17.1.54.
13 Jason Porath, "Amanirenas: The One-Eyed Queen Who Fought Rome Tooth and Nail," Rejected Princesses, 2020, https://www.rejectedprincesses.com/princesses/amanirenas.
14 Dio, Roman History, vol. 6, book 54, section 5.
15 Cristin O'Keefe Aptowicz, "Could You Stomach the Horrors of 'Halftime' in Ancient Rome?" livescience.com, February 4, 2016. https://www.livescience.com/53615-horrors-of-the-colosseum.html.
16 Dio, Roman History, vol. 6, book 54, section 5.
17 Magak, "One-Eyed African Queen."
18 Strabo, Geography of Strabo, 17.1.54.
19 O'Grady, And Man Created God, "The African Goddess-Queen."
20 Kai Mora, "The Nubian Queen Who Fought Back Caesar's Army," History, March 23, 2022, https://www.history.com/news/nubian-queen-amanirenas-roman-army.
21 Kamrin and Adela Oppenheim, "Land of Nubia."
22 Kamrin and Adela Oppenheim, "Land of Nubia."
23 Strabo, Geography of Strabo, 17.1.54.
24 Kamrin and Adela Oppenheim, "Land of Nubia."
25 Miriam Maat Ka Re Monges, "Kandakes, Ruling Queens of Ancient Meroe," in Molefi Kete Asante and Ama Mazama, ed., Encyclopedia of Black Studies (Thousand Oaks, CA: Sage, 2005), 302.
26 Mora, "Nubian Queen Who Fought Back."
27 David Francis, "The Meroë Head of Augustus: Statue Decapitation as Political Propaganda," British Museum, December 11, 2014, https://web.archive.org/web/20141231192911/https://blog.britishmuseum.org/2014/12/11/the-meroe-head-of-augustus-statue-decapitation-as-political-propaganda/.

Huang Chao

1 In Chinese names, the family name (here, Huang) is written first, and the given name (here, Chao) is written second.

2 Ray Huang, *China: A Macro History*, 2nd ed (Oxfordshire, UK: Routledge, 2015), https://perlego.com/book/1559230/china-a-macro-history-pdf.

3 Huang, *China*, 10. "The Second Empire: A Breakthrough That Failed to Materialize."

4 Huang, *China*, 10. "The Second Empire: A Breakthrough That Failed to Materialize."

5 Huang, *China*, 10. "The Second Empire: A Breakthrough That Failed to Materialize."

6 Mark Cartwright, "The Civil Service Examinations of Imperial China," World History Encyclopedia, February 8, 2019, https://www.worldhistory.org/article/1335/the-civil-service-examinations-of-imperial-china/.

7 Howard S. Levy, "Huang Ch'ao Ch'i-i [The Righteous Uprising of Huang Ch'ao]," *Journal of Asian Studies* 16, no. 4 (August 1957): 613. https://doi.org/10.2307/2941653.

8 Adam Fong, "Ending an Era: The Huang Chao Rebellion of the Late Tang, 874–884" (5th East-West Center Working Papers, International Graduate Student Conference Series, Honolulu, Hawaii, January 1, 2006), https://www.eastwestcenter.org/publications/ending-era-huang-chao-rebellion-late-tang-874-884.

9 Huang, *China*, 10. "The Second Empire: A Breakthrough That Failed to Materialize."

10 Levy, "Huang Ch'ao Ch'i-i," 616.

11 Levy, "Huang Ch'ao Ch'i-i," 614.

12 Levy, "Huang Ch'ao Ch'i-i," 614.

13 Huang, *China*, 10. "The Second Empire: A Breakthrough That Failed to Materialize."

14 Levy, "Huang Ch'ao Ch'i-i," 616.

15 Levy, "Huang Ch'ao Ch'i-i," 613.

16 Levy, "Huang Ch'ao Ch'i-i," 615.

17 Huang, *China*, 10. "The Second Empire: A Breakthrough That Failed to Materialize."

18 Huang, *China*, 10. "The Second Empire: A Breakthrough That Failed to Materialize."

19 Jonathan Clements, *A Brief History of China: Dynasty, Revolution and Transformation: From the Middle Kingdom to the People's Republic* (Clarendon, VT: Tuttle Publishing, 2019), 236, https://www.scribd.com/book/416290639/A-Brief-History-of-China-Dynasty-Revolution-and-Transformation-From-the-Middle-Kingdom-to-the-People-s-Republic.

20 Clements, *Brief History of China*, 237.

21 Clements, *Brief History of China*, 237.

22 Levy, "Huang Ch'ao Ch'i-i," 616.

23 Levy, "Huang Ch'ao Ch'i-i," 616.

24 Levy, "Huang Ch'ao Ch'i-i," 616.

25 Clements, *Brief History of China*, 237.

26 Levy, "Huang Ch'ao Ch'i-i," 612.

27 Levy, "Huang Ch'ao Ch'i-i," 612.

al-Sayyida al-Hurra

1 Sarah Williams, "The Story Behind the Many Shades of Morocco's Blue City," Culture Trip, September 2, 2021, https://theculturetrip.com/morocco/articles/the-story-behind-the-many-shades-of-moroccos-blue-city/.

2 Hasna Lebbady, "Women in Northern Morocco: Between the Documentary and the Imaginary," *Alif: Journal of Comparative Poetics* 32 (2012): 132. https://www.jstor.org/stable/41850741.

3 Lebbady, "Women in Northern Morocco," 131.

4 Adam Ali, "The Pirate Queen of the Mediterranean: The Story of Al-Sayyida al-Hurra," Medievalists.net, August 4, 2022, https://www.medievalists.net/2022/08/pirate-queen-mediterranean-al-sayyida-al-hurra/.

5 Lebbady, "Women in Northern Morocco," 132.

6 Ali, "Pirate Queen."

7 Laura Sook Duncombe, *Pirate Women: The Princesses, Prostitutes, and Privateers Who Ruled the Seven Seas* (Chicago: Chicago Review Press, 2019), 61.

8 Fatima Mernissi, *The Forgotten Queens of Islam* (Minneapolis: University of Minnesota Press, 2012), 19, http://archive.org/details/forgottenqueenso0000mern.

9 Ali, "Pirate Queen."

10 Duncombe, *Pirate Women*, 55.

11 Duncombe, *Pirate Women*, 56.

12 Duncombe, *Pirate Women*, 57.

13 Kallie Szczepanski, "Admiral Hayreddin Barbarossa," ThoughtCo, updated January 21, 2020, https://www.thoughtco.com/admiral-hayreddin-barbarossa-195756.

14 "The Fortifications of Gibraltar," Gibraltar National Museum, accessed January 29, 2023, https://www.gibmuseum.gi/our-history/military-history/fortifications-of-gibraltar.

15 Mernissi, *Forgotten Queens*, 193.

16 Mernissi, *Forgotten Queens*, 18.

17 Duncombe, *Pirate Women*, 62.

18 Mernissi, *Forgotten Queens*, 18.

19 Ali, "Pirate Queen."

20 Duncombe, *Pirate Women*, 62.

21 Ali, "Pirate Queen."

22 Mernissi, *Forgotten Queens*, 18.

23 Duncombe, *Pirate Women*, 62.

24 Duncombe, *Pirate Women*, 63.

25 Lebbady, "Women in Northern Morocco," 133.

26 Lebbady, "Women in Northern Morocco," 132.

27 Ali, "Pirate Queen."

28 Lebbady, "Women in Northern Morocco," 134.

29 Lebbady, "Women in Northern Morocco," 134.

30 Lebbady, "Women in Northern Morocco," 133.

31 Richard Boly, "The Allegory of California," Atlas Obscura, January 6, 2020, http://www.atlasobscura.com/places/the-allegory-of-california.

NOTES

Suleiman the Magnificent

1 Cornell H. Fleischer, "A Mediterranean Apocalypse: Prophecies of Empire in the Fifteenth and Sixteenth Centuries," *Journal of the Economic and Social History of the Orient* 61, no. 1/2 (2018): 19. https://www.jstor.org/stable/26572297.
2 Marc David Baer, *The Ottomans: Khans, Caesars, and Caliphs* (New York: Basic Books, 2021), 154.
3 André Clot, *Suleiman the Magnificent*, trans. Matthew Reisz (London: Saqi Books, 2012), 29.
4 Clot and Reisz, trans., *Suleiman the Magnificent*, 28.
5 Clot and Reisz, trans., *Suleiman the Magnificent*, 30.
6 Clot and Reisz, trans., *Suleiman the Magnificent*, 31.
7 Clot and Reisz, trans., *Suleiman the Magnificent*, 29.
8 Mike Dash, "The Ottoman Empire's Life-or-Death Race," *Smithsonian Magazine*, March 22, 2012, https://www.smithsonianmag.com/history/the-ottoman-empires-life-or-death-race-164064882/.
9 Baer, *The Ottomans*, 238.
10 Baer, *The Ottomans*, 238.
11 Clot and Reisz, trans., *Suleiman the Magnificent*, 48.
12 Baer, *The Ottomans*, 239.
13 Baer, *The Ottomans*, 241.
14 Baer, *The Ottomans*, 241.
15 Mark Cartwright, "The Hippodrome of Constantinople," World History Encyclopedia, November 28, 2017, https://www.worldhistory.org/article/1158/the-hippodrome-of-constantinople/.
16 Walter G. Andrews and Mehmet Kalpakli, *The Age of Beloveds: Love and the Beloved in Early-Modern Ottoman and European Culture and Society* (Durham, NC: Duke University Press, 2005), 239, https://www.perlego.com/book/1467351/the-age-of-beloveds-love-and-the-beloved-in-earlymodern-ottoman-and-european-culture-and-society-pdf.
17 Clot and Reisz, trans., *Suleiman the Magnificent*, 69.
18 Clot and Reisz, trans., *Suleiman the Magnificent*, 69.
19 Clot and Reisz, trans., *Suleiman the Magnificent*, 69.
20 Duncombe, *Pirate Women*, 63.
21 Duncombe, *Pirate Women*, 64.
22 Baer, *The Ottomans*, 235.
23 Clot and Reisz, trans., *Suleiman the Magnificent*, 70.
24 Duncombe, *Pirate Women*, 67.
25 Clot and Reisz, trans., *Suleiman the Magnificent*, 69.
26 Duncombe, *Pirate Women*, 67.
27 Clot and Reisz, trans., *Suleiman the Magnificent*, 94.
28 Baer, *The Ottomans*, 241.
29 Clot and Reisz, trans., *Suleiman the Magnificent*, 96.
30 Baer, *The Ottomans*, 241.
31 Clot and Reisz, trans., *Suleiman the Magnificent*, 96.
32 Baer, *The Ottomans*, 242.
33 Baer, *The Ottomans*, 242.
34 Duncombe, *Pirate Women*, 67.
35 Baer, *The Ottomans*, 173.

Aphra Behn

1 Janet Todd, *Aphra Behn: A Secret Life* (London: Fentum Press, 2017), xxvii. Unless otherwise noted, all quotes and facts in this chapter come from this publication.
2 Sister Mary Catherine McMahon, "The Astrée and Its Influence," *Catholic Historical Review* 12, no. 2 (1926): 228. https://www.jstor.org/stable/25012301.
3 Paul Salzman, "Introduction," in Aphra Behn, *Oroonoko and Other Writings*, Oxford World's Classics (Oxford, UK: Oxford University Press, 2009). Kindle.
4 Salzman, "Introduction," *Oroonoko and Other Writings*.
5 Ashley Chantler, "The Meaning of 'Scotch Fiddle' in Rochester's 'Tunbridge Wells,'" *Restoration: Studies in English Literary Culture, 1660–1700* 26, no. 2 (2002): 83. https://www.jstor.org/stable/43293724.
6 Salzman, "Introduction," *Oroonoko and Other Writings*.
7 Salzman, "Introduction," *Oroonoko and Other Writings*.
8 Aphra Behn, "To Lysander," Poetry Foundation, https://www.poetryfoundation.org/poems/50270/to-lysander.
9 The British Library. "Aphra Behn's Oroonoko, 1688." Accessed April 16, 2023. https://www.bl.uk/collection-items/aphra-behns-oroonoko-1688.

Toussaint L'Ouverture

1 Charles Forsdick and Christian Høgsbjerg, *Toussaint Louverture: A Black Jacobin in the Age of Revolutions* (London: Pluto Press, 2017), https://www.scribd.com/book/369360093/Toussaint-Louverture-A-Black-Jacobin-in-the-Age-of-Revolutions. Unless otherwise noted, all quotes and facts in this chapter come from this publication.
2 Arthur F. Saint-Aubin, "Editing Toussaint Louverture's Memoir: Representing Racial Difference," *French Review* 85, no. 4 (2012): 658. http://www.jstor.org/stable/23214721.
3 Marlene L. Daut, "The Wrongful Death of Toussaint Louverture," *History Today* 70 no. 6, June 6, 2020, https://www.historytoday.com/archive/feature/wrongful-death-toussaint-louverture.
4 Lauren Collins, "The Haitian Revolution and the Hole in French High-School History," *New Yorker*, December 3, 2020, https://www.newyorker.com/culture/culture-desk/the-haitian-revolution-and-the-hole-in-french-high-school-history.
5 John E. Fagg, "Toussaint Louverture," Britannica, last updated Nov 23, 2022, https://www.britannica.com/biography/Toussaint-Louverture.
6 Kedon Willis, "How Toussaint L'ouverture Rose from Slavery to Lead the Haitian Revolution," History, August 30, 2021, https://www.history.com/news/toussaint-louverture-haiti-revolution.
7 Collins, "Haitian Revolution."

8   John Relly Beard, *Toussaint L'Ouverture: A Biography and Autobiography* (Boston: J. Redpath, 1863), 188, https://www.google.com/books/edition/Toussaint_L_Ouverture/BPYCAAAAYAAJ?hl=en&gbpv=0.
9   Daut, "Wrongful Death."
10 Daut, "Wrongful Death."
11 Daut, "Wrongful Death."
12 Daut, "Wrongful Death."

Raḥmah ibn Jābir al-Jalāhimah
1   "Arabian Horses Spread to Europe," Trowbridge's, accessed April 16, 2023, https://www.trowbridgesltd.com/arabian-horses-spread-to-europe/.
2   "The Scourge of the Pirate Coast: Rahmah bin Jaber," Qatar Visitor, July 15, 2011. https://web.archive.org/web/20110715134241/http://www.qatarvisitor.com/index.php?cID=430&pID=1382.
3   Charles Belgrave, *The Pirate Coast*, 2nd ed. (Beirut: Librarie du Liban, 1960), 75, https://online.flipbuilder.com/kiwg/sixg/. Unless otherwise noted, all quotes and facts in this chapter come from this publication.
4   James Silk Buckingham, *Travels in Assyria, Media, and Persia* (London: H. Colburn, 1829), 356, http://archive.org/details/travelsinassyri00buckgoog.
5   Buckingham, *Travels in Assyria*, 356–7.
6   Geoffrey King, "Islamic Architecture in Eastern Arabia," *Proceedings of the Seminar for Arabian Studies* 8 (1978): 21.

Manuela Sáenz
1   Pamela S. Murray, *For Glory and Bolívar: The Remarkable Life of Manuela Sáenz* (Austin: University of Texas Press, 2008), 9. Unless otherwise noted, all quotes and facts in this chapter come from this publication.
2   James Higgins, *Lima: A Cultural History*, Cityscapes (Oxford, UK: Oxford University Press, 2005), 86.
3   Higgins, *Lima*, 86.
4   Higgins, *Lima*, 87.
5   Robert B. McAfee, "Letter from Robert B. McAfee in Bogotá to U.S. Secretary of State, Louis McClane, in Washington, D.C.," January 19, 1834, Despatches from U.S. Ministers to Colombia, 1820–1906, U.S. National Archives, microfilm, roll 8, https://catalog.archives.gov/id/189276212?objectPage=90.
6   Pamela S. Murray, "'Loca' or 'Libertadora'?: Manuela Sáenz in the Eyes of History and Historians, 1900–c. 1990," *Journal of Latin American Studies* 33, no. 2 (2001): 292. https://www.jstor.org/stable/3653686.
7   "Nuestra Historia Y Quiénes Somos," Museo Manuela Sáenz, accessed February 3, 2023, https://museo-manuela-saenz.negocio.site.

Tarenorerer
1   Lyndall Ryan, *Tasmanian Aborigines: A History Since 1803* (Sydney: Allen & Unwin, 2012), 80. Unless otherwise noted, all quotes and facts in this chapter come from this publication.
2   Shane Carroll, "Ochre Is of the Earth," Bangarra Dance Theatre Knowledge Ground, accessed February 11, 2023, https://bangarra-knowledgeground.com.au/productions/ochres/ochre-is-of-the-earth.
3   Vicki maikutena Matson-Green, "Tarenorerer (1800–1831)," in *Australian Dictionary of Biography: Supplement 1580–1980*, ed. Christopher Cunneen (Carlton: Melbourne University Press, 2005), https://adb.anu.edu.au/biography/tarenorerer-13212.
4   Matson-Green, "Tarenorerer."
5   Matson-Green, "Tarenorerer."
6   Matson-Green, "Tarenorerer."
7   "Aboriginal Burials" Aboriginal Heritage Tasmania, Tasmanian Government, November 8, 2017, https://www.aboriginalheritage.tas.gov.au/cultural-heritage/aboriginal-burials.
8   Matson-Green, "Tarenorerer."
9   Andrew Bain, "The Rebirth of Tasmanian Indigenous Culture," Travel, BBC, October 25, 2021, https://www.bbc.com/travel/article/20211024-the-rebirth-of-tasmanian-indigenous-culture.

Henry Dunant
1   Corinne Chaponnière, *Henry Dunant: The Man of the Red Cross*, trans. Michelle Bailat-Jones (London: Bloomsbury Publishing, 2022), "A Little Aristocrat," Perlego. https://ereader.perlego.com/1/book/3046431/10.
2   Chaponnière, *Henry Dunant*, "Happy Times."
3   Chaponnière, *Henry Dunant*, "The Happy Eldest."
4   Chaponnière, *Henry Dunant*, "The Narrow Door."
5   Chaponnière, *Henry Dunant*, "A Little Aristocrat."
6   Chaponnière, *Henry Dunant*, "The Young Men's Christian Association."
7   Chaponnière, *Henry Dunant*, "A Faraway Mission."
8   Chaponnière, *Henry Dunant*, "Making His Mark."
9   Chaponnière, *Henry Dunant*, "Scientific Ambitions."
10 J. Henry Dunant, *Notice sur la régence de Tunis* (Geneva: Fick, 1858), 186, http://archive.org/details/bub_gb_JakBAAAAQAAJ.
11 Chaponnière, *Henry Dunant*, "A Bow to the Emperor."
12 Chaponnière, *Henry Dunant*, "A Fateful Meeting in Italy."
13 Mike Vuolo, "Let's Resolve in the New Year to Stop Using That Expression About Breaking Eggs and Making Omelets," *Slate*, December 30, 2013, https://slate.com/human-interest/2013/12/english-idioms-it-may-be-true-that-you-can-t-make-an-omelet-without-breaking-eggs-but-please-stop-saying-that.html.
14 Chaponnière, *Henry Dunant*, "The Battle of Solferino."
15 Chaponnière, *Henry Dunant*, "The Battle of Solferino."
16 J. Henry Dunant, *A Memory of Solferino*, trans. American National Red Cross (London: Cassell, 1947), 21, http://archive.org/details/b29978877.

17 Chaponnière, *Henry Dunant*, "The Battle of Solferino."
18 Chaponnière, *Henry Dunant*, "The Battle of Solferino."
19 Chaponnière, *Henry Dunant*, "The Battle of Solferino."
20 Chaponnière, *Henry Dunant*, "Tutti Fratelli."
21 Chaponnière, *Henry Dunant*, "Tutti Fratelli."
22 Dunant, *Solferino*, 35.
23 Chaponnière, *Henry Dunant*, "Writing A Memory."
24 Dunant, *Solferino*, 115.
25 Chaponnière, *Henry Dunant*, "The Publication."
26 Chaponnière, *Henry Dunant*, "One Congress Is Worth Another."
27 Chaponnière, *Henry Dunant*, "The Conference of October 1863."
28 Chaponnière, *Henry Dunant*, "The Conference of October 1863."
29 "Swiss Flag," Discover Switzerland, updated March 15, 2022, https://www.eda.admin.ch/aboutswitzerland/en/home/gesellschaft/traditionen/fahne.html.
30 Chaponnière, *Henry Dunant*, "The Bankruptcy."
31 Chaponnière, *Henry Dunant*, "Nostalgia for Activism."
32 Chaponnière, *Henry Dunant*, "Nostalgia for Activism."
33 "History," Nobel Peace Prize, August 26, 2021, https://www.nobelpeaceprize.org/nobel-peace-prize/history/.
34 "Henry Dunant (1828–1910)," International Committee of the Red Cross, April 6, 1998, https://www.icrc.org/en/doc/resources/documents/misc/57jnvq.htm.
35 Chaponnière, *Henry Dunant*, "The Ultimate Rival."

Sun Yat-sen

1 Tjio Kayloe, *The Unfinished Revolution: Sun Yat-Sen and the Struggle for Modern China* (Singapore: Marshall Cavendish, 2018). Unless otherwise noted, all quotes and facts in this chapter come from this publication.
2 Marie-Claire Bergère, *Sun Yat-sen*, trans. Janet Lloyd (Stanford, California: Stanford University Press, 2000), 49.
3 Clements, *Brief History of China*, 395.
4 Yi Chu Wang, "The Revolution of 1911," Sun Yat-sen; Presidents & Heads of State; World Leaders; Politics, Law & Government; Britannica, January 23, 2023, https://www.britannica.com/biography/Sun-Yat-sen/The-revolution-of-1911.
5 Clements, *Brief History of China*, 395.
6 Sun Yat-Sen, *Memoirs of a Chinese Revolutionary* (Philadelphia: David McKay, 1918), 220, https://www.scribd.com/document/466761032/Sun-Yat-Sen-Memoirs-of-a-Chinese-Revolutionary-pdf.
7 Sun, *Memoirs*, 221.
8 Bergère, *Sun Yat-sen*, 211.
9 Bergère, *Sun Yat-sen*, 211.
10 Sun Yat Sen, "'My Reminiscences,' The Strand Magazine, 1912a Vol. XLIII, Jan-Jun," in *Collection of Bound Editions of The Strand Magazine: An Illustrated Monthly*, ed. George Newnes (London: The Strand Magazine, 1891), http://archive.org/details/TheStrandMagazineAnIllustratedMonthly.

Mary Moloney

1 "Glasthule Baptisms: May 27th 1865 to December 24th 1902," Catholic Parish Registers at the NLI, National Library of Ireland, accessed May 15, 2022, http://registers.nli.ie/parishes/0522.
2 *Suffragettes Forever! The Story of Women and Power*, episode 2, "Episode 1.2" directed by Rupert Edwards, written by Jacqui Hayden, aired March 4, 2015 on BBC.
3 Ray Strachey, *The Cause: A Short History of the Women's Movement in Great Britain* (Port Washington, NY: Kennikat Press, 1969), 301, http://archive.org/details/causeshorthistor0083stra.
4 Strachey, *The Cause*, 301.
5 National Federation of Women Workers, "Gaps in the Grille," *The Woman Worker*, November 4, 1908.
6 *Suffragettes Forever!*
7 "Dundee Election: Mr. Churchill and the Suffragettes: Amusing Scenes: Silenced by a Clanging Bell," *Irish Times*, May 5, 1908, https://www.britishnewspaperarchive.co.uk/viewer/bl/0001683/19080505/138/0005.
8 "Dundee Election."
9 "Dundee Election."
10 "Dundee Election."
11 "Dundee Election."
12 "Dundee Election."
13 "Dundee Election."
14 "Dundee Election."
15 "Dundee Election."
16 "Dundee Election."
17 "House of Commons General View, Showing the Ladies' Gallery above the Speaker's Chair" (United Kingdom Parliament), Parliamentary Archives, FAR/1/7, UK Living Heritage, accessed April 13, 2023, https://www.parliament.uk/about/living-heritage/transformingsociety/electionsvoting/womenvote/parliamentary-collections/ladies-gallery-grille/ladies-gallery/.
18 Women Workers, "Gaps in the Grille."
19 Women Workers, "Gaps in the Grille."
20 "Who Were the Suffragettes?," Museum of London, May 15, 2022, https://www.museumoflondon.org.uk/museum-london/explore/who-were-suffragettes.
21 Eleanor Wallace, "Suffragette Outrages: The Women's Social and Political Union WSPU," Historic UK, February 10, 2022, https://www.historic-uk.com/HistoryUK/HistoryofBritain/Suffragette-Outrages-WSPU/.
22 Josh Clark and Chuck Bryant, "What Were the IRA Hunger Strikes?," June 16, 2022, in *Stuff You Should Know*, podcast, MP3 audio, 50 min., https://www.iheart.com/podcast/105-stuff-you-should-know-26940277/episode/what-were-the-ira-hunger-strikes-98402100/.
23 "Who Were the Suffragettes?"
24 "Suffragettes Bomb Westminster Abbey," *Raidió Teilifís Éireann*, June 12, 1914, Century Ireland, https://www.rte.ie/centuryireland/index.php/articles/suffragettes-bomb-westminster-abbey.
25 Representation of the People Act, 1918, United Kingdom Parliament (February 6, 1918), UK Living Heritage, https://www.parliament.uk/about/living-heritage/transformingsociety/electionsvoting/womenvote/case-study-the-right-to-vote/

the-right-to-vote/birmingham-and-the-equal-fran-chise/1918-representation-of-the-people-act/.
26 *Suffragettes Forever!*
27 "In Memoriam: Horatia Dorothy Molony Lancaster," *The Vote*, December 9, 1921, British Newspapers Archive, https://www.britishnewspaperarchive.co.uk/viewer/bl/0002186/19211209/016/0006.

Amelio Robles Ávila

1   In Spanish names, the first surname (here, Robles) is the paternal family name, and the second surname is the maternal family name (here, Ávila). It's traditional to refer to Latine people by the paternal family name.
2   Laura Martinez Alarcón, "La Coronela es un hombre y, sin embargo, nació mujer," Actitudfem, March 7, 2016, https://www.actitudfem.com/entorno/genero/lgbt/la-coronela-es-un-hombre-y-sin-embargo-nacio-mujer.
3   Gabriela Cano, "Unconcealable Realities of Desire," in *Sex in Revolution: Gender, Politics, and Power in Modern Mexico*, ed. Jocelyn Olcott, Mary Kay Vaughan, and Gabriela Cano (Durham, NC: Duke University Press, 2007), 43. Unless otherwise noted, all quotes and facts in this chapter come from this publication.
4   Martinez Alarcón, "La Coronela es un hombre."
5   Emiliano Zapata and Otilio Montaño, "Plan of Ayala," November 25, 1911, Library of Congress, https://www.loc.gov/item/2021667593/.
6   Martinez Alarcón, "La Coronela es un hombre."
7   Martinez Alarcón, "La Coronela es un hombre."
8   Martinez Alarcón, "La Coronela es un hombre."
9   Carlos Monsiváis, "Foreword," in *Sex in Revolution: Gender, Politics, and Power in Modern Mexico*, ed. Jocelyn Olcott, Mary Kay Vaughan, and Gabriela Cano (Durham, NC: Duke University Press, 2007), 10.
10 Martinez Alarcón, "La Coronela es un hombre."

Joe Carstairs

1   Kate Summerscale, *The Queen of Whale Cay: The Eccentric Story of "Joe" Carstairs, Fastest Woman on Water* (New York: Viking, 1998), 18, http://archive.org/details/queenofwhalecay0000summ_h8z4.
2   Summerscale, *Queen of Whale Cay*, 24.
3   Summerscale, *Queen of Whale Cay*, 40.
4   Summerscale, *Queen of Whale Cay*, 56.
5   Summerscale, *Queen of Whale Cay*, 60.
6   Summerscale, *Queen of Whale Cay*, 59.
7   Summerscale, *Queen of Whale Cay*, 90.
8   D. Clark, "Population of the United Kingdom from 1871 to 2021," Statista, accessed February 1, 2023, https://www.statista.com/statistics/281296/uk-population/.
9   "The Duke of York's Trophy Motor-boat Races.," *Motor Sport Magazine* (September 1927), 70. https://www.motorsportmaga-zine.com/archive/article/september-1927/12/the-duke-of-yorks-trophy-motor-boat-races/.
10 Summerscale, *Queen of Whale Cay*, 70.
11 Summerscale, *Queen of Whale Cay*, 72.
12 Summerscale, *Queen of Whale Cay*, 71.
13 Summerscale, *Queen of Whale Cay*, 84.

14 Summerscale, *Queen of Whale Cay*, 104.
15 Summerscale, *Queen of Whale Cay*, 114.
16 Summerscale, *Queen of Whale Cay*, 122.
17 Summerscale, *Queen of Whale Cay*, 129.
18 West Indies: Volume 331: Debated on Wednesday 9 February 1938, Hansard, UK Parliament, https://hansard.parliament.uk//Commons/1938-02-09/debates/3e35d447-101a-4eab-91b8-3081ef6a179e/WestIndies.
19 Summerscale, *Queen of Whale Cay*, 155.
20 Summerscale, *Queen of Whale Cay*, 169.
21 Eric T. Wiberg, "S. S. *Potlatch* and Capt. John Joseph Lapoint," September 16, 2015, https://www.academia.edu/25038931/BHS_FINAL_Article_SS_Potlatch_by_ET_Wiberg.

Witold Pilecki

1   Ewa Cuber-Strutyńska, "Witold Pilecki: Confronting the Legend of the 'Volunteer to Auschwitz,'" in "Holocaust Studies and Materials, vol. 4 of *Journal of the Polish Center for Holocaust Research* (December 6, 2017): 282, https://doi.org/10.32927/zzsim.720.
2   Jarek Garliński, "Historical Horizon," in *The Auschwitz Volunteer: Beyond Bravery*, Kindle (Aquila Polonica, 2014).
3   Garliński, "Historical Horizon."
4   Cuber-Strutyńska, "Witold Pilecki," 283.
5   Cuber-Strutyńska, "Witold Pilecki," 283.
6   Garliński, "Historical Horizon."
7   Cuber-Strutyńska, "Witold Pilecki," 283.
8   Jozef Garliński, *Fighting Auschwitz: The Resistance Movement in the Concentration Camp* (Los Angeles: Aquila Polonica, 1975), 60.
9   Jack Fairweather, *The Volunteer: One Man, an Underground Army, and the Secret Mission to Destroy Auschwitz* (New York, NY: Custom House, 2019), "Occupation," Kindle.
10 Garliński, *Fighting Auschwitz*, 60.
11 Fairweather, *The Volunteer*, "Occupation."
12 Fairweather, *The Volunteer*, "Occupation."
13 Fairweather, *The Volunteer*, "Occupation."
14 Fairweather, *The Volunteer*, "Occupation."
15 Fairweather, *The Volunteer*, "Occupation."
16 Pilecki, Witold. *The Auschwitz Volunteer: Beyond Bravery.* Translated by Jarek Garliński. Kindle. Aquila Polonica, 2014.
17 Cuber-Strutyńska, "Witold Pilecki," 289.
18 Pilecki, *Auschwitz Volunteer*, 146.
19 Pilecki, *Auschwitz Volunteer*, 36.
20 Pilecki, *Auschwitz Volunteer*, 36.
21 Garliński, *Fighting Auschwitz*, 45.
22 Garliński, *Fighting Auschwitz*, 47.
23 Garliński, *Fighting Auschwitz*, 48.
24 Pilecki, *Auschwitz Volunteer*, 320.
25 Pilecki, *Auschwitz Volunteer*, 317.
26 Pilecki, *Auschwitz Volunteer*, 325.
27 Karol Wołek, "A Post-War War: The Years of 1944–1963 in Poland," *Warsaw Institute Review*, October 1, 2018, https://warsawinstitute.org/post-war-war-years-1944-1963-poland/.
28 Wołek, "Post-War War."

NOTES

29 "Captain Witold Pilecki," Instytut Pamięci Narodowej, accessed April 10, 2023, https://biogramy.ipn.gov.pl/bio/wszystkie-biogramy/rotmistrz-witold-pileck/english-version/112337,Captain-Witold-Pilecki.html.
30 Garliński, "Historical Horizon."
31 Garliński, "Historical Horizon."
32 Garliński, "Historical Horizon."
33 "Captain Witold Pilecki," Instytut Pamięci Narodowej.

Countée Cullen

1 Houston A. Baker, *Afro-American Poetics: Revisions of Harlem and the Black Aesthetic* (Madison: University of Wisconsin Press, 1988), 47.
2 Baker, *Afro-American Poetics*, 56.
3 Baker, *Afro-American Poetics*, 56.
4 Baker, *Afro-American Poetics*, 56.
5 Joanne Diaz and Abram Van Engen, "Countee Cullen, Yet Do I Marvel," episode 28, September 29, 2021, in *Poetry for All*, podcast, MP3 audio, 24:48, https://poetry-forall.fireside.fm/28.
6 Diaz and Van Engen, "Countee Cullen."
7 Countee Cullen, *Caroling Dusk: An Anthology of Verse by Negro Poets* (New York: NY: Harper & Brothers, 1927), xi–xii. https://archive.org/details/carolingdusk00coun/page/n11/mode/2up
8 Cullen, *Caroling Dusk*, xi.
9 Major Jackson, introduction to *Countee Cullen: Collected Poems, by Countee Cullen*, American Poets Project 32 (New York: Library of America, 2013), xxx.
10 Baker, *Afro-American Poetics*, 57.
11 "Overview." W. E. B. Du Bois Papers, 1803–1999 (bulk 1877–1963). Robert S. Cox Special Collections and University Archives Research Center. University of Massachusetts Amherst. Accessed February 13, 2023. https://credo.library.umass.edu/view/collection/mums312.
12 David L. Lewis, *When Harlem Was in Vogue*, 2nd edition (New York: Penguin Books, 1997), 203.
13 Lewis, *When Harlem Was in Vogue*, 203.
14 Lewis, *When Harlem Was in Vogue*, 203.
15 Baker, *Afro-American Poetics*, 57.
16 Yolande Du Bois to W. E. B. Du Bois, May 23, 1929, W. E. B. Du Bois Papers (MS 312), Special Collections and University Archives, University of Massachusetts Amherst Libraries, http://credo.library.umass.edu/view/full/mums312-b048-i062.
17 Yolande Du Bois to W. E. B. Du Bois.
18 "Countee Cullen," National Museum of African American History and Culture, accessed March 28, 2022, https://nmaahc.si.edu/countee-cullen.
19 Mason Stokes, "Strange Fruits," *Transition* 92 (2002): 58. https://www.jstor.org/stable/3172461.
20 Jackson, introduction to *Countee Cullen*, pg xx.
21 Jackson, introduction to *Countee Cullen*, pg xx.
22 Genny Beemyn, *A Queer Capital: A History of Gay Life in Washington D.C.* (Oxfordshire: Routledge, 2014), https://www.perlego.com/book/1545531/a-queer-capital-a-history-of-gay-life-in-washington-dc-pdf.
23 Beemyn, *Queer Capital*, "'Sentiments Expressed Here Would Be Misconstrued by Others.'"
24 Baker, *Afro-American Poetics*, 57.

Jonas Salk

1 Charlotte DeCroes Jacobs, *Jonas Salk: A Life* (New York: Oxford University Press, 2015), 3. Unless otherwise noted, all quotes and facts in this chapter come from this publication.
2 Bali Pulendran, Prabhu S. Arunachalam, and Derek T. O'Hagan, "Emerging Concepts in the Science of Vaccine Adjuvants," *Nature Reviews Drug Discovery* 20, no. 6 (June 2021): 454, https://doi.org/10.1038/s41573-021-00163-y.
3 "Adjuvants and Vaccines," Questions and Concerns, Vaccine Safety, Centers for Disease Control and Prevention, updated September 27, 2022, https://www.cdc.gov/vaccinesafety/concerns/adjuvants.html.
4 "About Jonas Salk," Salk Institute for Biological Studies, accessed June 12, 2022, https://www.salk.edu/about/history-of-salk/jonas-salk/.
5 "About Jonas Salk."
6 Marcia Meldrum, "'A Calculated Risk': The Salk Polio Vaccine Field Trials of 1954," *British Medical Journal* 317, no. 7167 (October 31, 1998): 1233.
7 *The Open Mind*, episode "Man Evolving," aired May 11, 1985 on PBS, https://www.njpbs.org/programs/the-open-mind/the-open-mind-man-evolving/.
8 Howard Taubman, "Father of Biophilosophy," *New York Times*, November 11, 1966.
9 "About Jonas Salk."
10 "About Jonas Salk."
11 "About Jonas Salk."

Sturtevant

1 Margalit Fox, "Elaine Sturtevant, Who Borrowed Others' Work Artfully, Is Dead at 89," *New York Times*, May 16, 2014, https://www.nytimes.com/2014/05/17/arts/design/elaine-sturtevant-appropriation-art-ist-is-dead-at-89.html.
2 "Trends: Statements in Paint," *Time*, February 28, 1969, https://content.time.com/time/subscriber/article/0,33009,900703-3,00.html.
3 Fox, "Elaine Sturtevant."
4 Patricia Lee, *Sturtevant: Warhol Marilyn*, One Work 14 (London: Afterall Books, 2016), 14.
5 Lee, *Sturtevant*, 14.
6 Peter Eleey and Elaine Sturtevant, *Sturtevant: Double Trouble* (New York: Museum of Modern Art, 2014), 50.
7 Eleey and Sturtevant, *Sturtevant*, 50.
8 Eleey and Sturtevant, *Sturtevant*, 50.
9 "Sturtevant with Peter Halley," *Index* (2005), http://www.indexmagazine.com/interviews/sturtevant.shtml.
10 Dea K., "Elaine Sturtevant," Widewalls, August 30, 2016, https://www.widewalls.ch/artists/elaine-sturtevant.
11 *Sturtevant's Repetitions*, Museum of Contemporary Art, 2015, YouTube video, 3:30, https://www.youtube.com/watch?v=PMhjxwR_-KY.
12 Eleey and Sturtevant, *Sturtevant*, 50.
13 Fox, "Elaine Sturtevant."
14 Eleey and Sturtevant, *Sturtevant*, 49.
15 Eleey and Sturtevant, *Sturtevant*, 47.
16 Eleey and Sturtevant, *Sturtevant*, 49.
17 Eleey and Sturtevant, *Sturtevant*, 49.

18 Lee, *Sturtevant*, 13.
19 Lee, *Sturtevant*, 15.
20 "Trends: Statements in Paint."
21 Eleanor Heartney, "Re-Creating Sturtevant," *Art in America* (November 1, 2014), https://www.artnews.com/art-in-america/features/re-creating-sturtevant-63492/.
22 Lee, *Sturtevant*, 12.
23 Lee, *Sturtevant*, 12.
24 Heartney, "Re-Creating Sturtevant."
25 Heartney, "Re-Creating Sturtevant."
26 Heartney, "Re-Creating Sturtevant."
27 Heartney, "Re-Creating Sturtevant."
28 "Sturtevant with Peter Halley."
29 Sturtevant, *Oral History Interview with Elaine Sturtevant, 2007 July 25–26*, 2007, Archives of American Art, Smithsonian Institution, https://www.aaa.si.edu/collections/interviews/oral-history-interview-elaine-sturtevant-13622.
30 "Sturtevant (1926–2014) *Lichtenstein, Frighten Girl*," Post-War & Contemporary Art Evening Sale, Live Auction 2891, Christie's, November 11, 2014, https://www.christies.com/en/lot/lot-5846086.
31 Fox, "Elaine Sturtevant."

Stanislav Petrov
1 *The Man Who Saved the World*, directed by Peter Anthony, docudrama (2015), https://www.amazon.com/Man-Who-Saved-World/dp/B07DVVKFTW.
2 Simon Shuster, "Stanislav Petrov, the Russian Officer Who Averted a Nuclear War, Feared History Repeating Itself," *Time*, September 19, 2017, https://time.com/4947879/stanislav-petrov-russia-nuclear-war-obituary/.
3 David Hoffman, "I Had A Funny Feeling in My Gut," *Washington Post*, February 10, 1999, https://web.archive.org/web/20181218193954/https://www.washingtonpost.com/wp-srv/inatl/longterm/coldwar/soviet10.htm.
4 "Korean Air Lines Flight 007," Britannica, last updated February 3, 2023, https://www.britannica.com/event/Korean-Air-Lines-flight-007.
5 "Korean Air Lines Flight 007."
6 "Korean Air Lines Flight 007."
7 Allan Little, "How I Stopped Nuclear War," BBC News, October 21, 1998, https://web.archive.org/web/20061108234104/http://news.bbc.co.uk/2/hi/europe/198173.stm.
8 Pavel Aksenov, "Stanislav Petrov: The Man Who May Have Saved the World," BBC News, September 26, 2013, https://web.archive.org/web/20140308000459/https://www.bbc.com/news/world-europe-24280831.
9 Aksenov, "Stanislav Petrov."
10 Hoffman, "I Had A Funny Feeling."
11 Sewell Chan, "Stanislav Petrov, Soviet Officer Who Helped Avert Nuclear War, Is Dead at 77," *New York Times*, September 18, 2017, https://web.archive.org/web/20170919023131/https://www.nytimes.com/2017/09/18/world/europe/stanislav-petrov-nuclear-war-dead.html.

12 *The Man Who Saved the World*.
13 *The Man Who Saved the World*.
14 Hoffman, "I Had A Funny Feeling."
15 Hoffman, "I Had A Funny Feeling."
16 *The Man Who Saved the World*.
17 Hoffman, "I Had A Funny Feeling."
18 Shuster, "Stanislav Petrov."
19 *The Man Who Saved the World*.
20 *The Man Who Saved the World*.
21 *The Man Who Saved the World*.
22 Hoffman, "I Had A Funny Feeling."
23 *The Man Who Saved the World*.
24 Glen Pedersen, "Stanislav Petrov: World Hero," *Fellowship* 71 no. 7–8 (July 2005): 9.
25 Little, "'How I Stopped Nuclear War.'"
26 Anastasiya Lebedev, "The Man Who Saved the World Finally Recognized," Association of World Citizens, May 21, 2004, https://web.archive.org/web/20110721000030/http://www.worldcitizens.org/petrov2.html.
27 Little, "How I Stopped Nuclear War."
28 Chan, "Stanislav Petrov."
29 Little, "'How I Stopped Nuclear War.'"
30 *The Man Who Saved the World*.
31 Chan, "Stanislav Petrov."
32 Shuster, "Stanislav Petrov."
33 *The Man Who Saved the World*.
34 *The Man Who Saved the World*.
35 Chan, "Stanislav Petrov."
36 Chan, "Stanislav Petrov."
37 *The Man Who Saved the World*.

Wangari Maathai
1 Jenni Murray, *A History of the World in 21 Women: A Personal Selection* (London: Oneworld Publications, 2018), 203, Scribd. https://www.scribd.com/book/433020639/A-History-of-the-World-in-21-Women-A-Personal-Selection.
2 Murray, "Wangari Maathai," 206.
3 Tabitha Kanogo, *Wangari Maathai*, Ohio Short Histories of Africa (Athens: Ohio University Press, 2020), 25, https://www.scribd.com/book/453420977/Wangari-Maathai.
4 Kanogo, *Wangari Maathai*, 27.
5 Wangari Maathai, *Unbowed: A Memoir* (New York: Alfred A. Knopf, 2006), 61, https://archive.org/details/unbowedmemoir0000maat/.
6 "Ghettos," Holocaust Encyclopedia, United States Holocaust Memorial Museum, accessed February 15, 2023, https://encyclopedia.ushmm.org/content/en/article/ghettos.
7 Wangari Maathai, "Bottlenecks to Development in Africa" (4th UN World Women's Conference, Beijing, China, August 30, 1995), https://www.greenbeltmovement.org/wangari-maathai/key-speeches-and-articles/bottleknecks-to-development-in-africa.
8 Murray, "Wangari Maathai," 210.
9 Maathai, "Bottlenecks to Development," 146.
10 Murray, "Wangari Maathai," 208.

11 *Taking Root: The Vision of Wangari Maathai,* BrattleboroTV2, 2008, YouTube video, 1:20:00, https://www.youtube.com/watch?v=G3My-B4NtOI.
12 *Taking Root.*
13 Kanogo, *Wangari Maathai,* 99.
14 Kanogo, *Wangari Maathai,* 99.
15 Kanogo, *Wangari Maathai,* 107.
16 Kanogo, *Wangari Maathai,* 101.
17 *Taking Root.*
18 Kanogo, *Wangari Maathai,* 93.
19 Kanogo, *Wangari Maathai,* 96.
20 *Taking Root.*
21 *Taking Root.*
22 *Taking Root.*
23 Kanogo, *Wangari Maathai,* 117.
24 Wangari Maathai, "Nobel Lecture" (Nobel Peace Prize 2004, Oslo, Norway, December 10, 2004), https://www.nobelprize.org/prizes/peace/2004/maathai/lecture/.

PUBLISHED BY
Princeton Architectural Press
A division of Chronicle Books LLC
70 West 36th Street
New York, NY 10018
papress.com

ISBN 978-1-7972-2363-6

ILLUSTRATIONS: Sam Kostka
EDITOR: Holly La Due
DESIGNER: Paul Wagner

Library of Congress Control Number: 2023941590